Earth does not belong to the man. Man belongs to the earth.

Chief of India Seatle - 1854

George Sfikas

Birds and Mammals of Crete

ATHENS

Efstathiadis Group S.A.
Agiou Athanasiou Street
GR - 145 65 Anixi, Attikis

ISBN 960 226 105 6

© Efstathiadis Group S.A. 1994

Printed and bound in Greece by Efstathiadis Group S.A.

INTRODUCTION

Crete is the second largest Greek island, after the Peloponnese, and one of the largest islands in the Mediterranean basin, with an area of 8.331 square kilometres. Its mild climate,
beautiful beaches, sunny weather and famous agricultural products have made Crete widely known throughout the world. But aside from the above attributes, Crete is also Famous for its unique natural world, characterised by a large variety of natural habitats as
well as by a large number of species of flora and fauna.

In this book we deal with the fauna of Crete and in particular the mammals and birds, two
classes of animals which have been sufficiently studied and for which the required data
exist. For the other classes, such as the reptiles, insects, molluscs, amphibians, etc., but
also for the animals living in the seas around Crete, the published data are so insufficient
that any such attempt would be doomed to failure. Besides, these classes include a very
large number of species and it would be difficult to fit them all into a single book.

In any case, today there is an urgent need for the classification and study of the fauna of
Crete, as there is for research into the condition of species populations. Unfortunately, all
the indications to date lead one to the conclusion that the populations of most species are
being reduced at a rapid pace. This is due to the destruction of natural habitats, to ruth-
less hunting and to the use of insecticides and herbicides in agriculture. In these circum-
stances it is not at all strange that since World War II, twenty-five species of birds have disappeared from Crete.

There is no doubt that in recent years Crete's natural environment has been severely un-
dermined by human activity, and that drastic measures must be taken to protect it. These
might include limitation of grazing to certain areas, reforestation of high mountains, a ban
of spraying from airplanes, the prohibition of hunting in certain important wetlands and
the creation of large wildlife preserves, where no hunting would be allowed. For the present, the only positive step which has been taken to protect wildlife in Crete has been the
creation of the White Mountains National Park, which includes the Samaria Gorge and
the surrounding peaks.

GEOLOGICAL PAST

Crete's geological past is full of upheavals. Twenty six million years ago, at the beginning
of the Meiocene, a continuous landmass rose out of the sea in the Aegean area. This
landmass, known as Aegeis, linked the peninsula of Greece with Asia Minor. Crete was
the southernmost part of Aegeis, and was therefore linked to Europe as well as to Asia.

During the middle Meiocene, about 18 million years ago, Aegeis was full of high
mountains. There were, however, also inland basis - depressions filled with fresh water.
During this period Crete continued to be linked to the neighbouring continents.

Towards the end of the Tertiary period, about 10 million years ago, Aegeis began to
change in form, as large sections of old land sank and the Mediterranean penetrated
deeper and deeper, creating the Aegean Sea. Geological upheavals continued during the
Pleiocene, 1-3 million years ago. It was then that Crete started to take on its present

shape, although it continued for some time to be divided into several smaller islands.

At the beginning of the Pleistocene, one million years ago, Crete was more or less as it is today in form. Geological upheavals continued to take place during the Pleistocene (1.000.000 -25.000 years ago) but they were much weaker and did not change the shape of the island to any great degree.

During the Pleistocene the climate of the earth changed many times. Periods of intense cold, much colder than earth's climate today, were followed by periods as warm as or warmer than our present climate. In one million years but planet passed through four Ice Ages and four interglacial periods. We are now in the fourth of these interglacial periods. During each Ice Age the level of the world's seas fell by hundreds of meters, as huge amounts of water were caught up in the form of ice. It is consequently probable that during those ages land bridges were created in the Aegean, thanks to which Crete may have been reunited with the neighbouring continental masses (Europe, Asia and Africa), as well as with the Cyclades.

PREHISTORIC MAMMALS OF CRETE

The existence of many species of mammals in crete in prehistoric times proves that it was at some time connected to neighbouring landmasses, although we are not in a position to know exactly when and how many ties such a connection came about, nor of what duration it was each time. Towards the end of the Meiocene (17 million years ago), large herbivorous mammals such as elephants, hippopotami, etc. lived in Crete. During the Pleistocene the island was full of many species of mammals, such as the pygmy Hippopotamus pentlandii, the wild cow (Bos primigenius), the deer-like Anaglochis cretensis, the wild goat Capra Aegagrus, a species of bison and pygmy elephants.

THE CRETAN ENVIRONMENT IN ANTIQUITY

During the Minoan era (2000-1100 B.C.) the environment in Crete was very different from what it is today. The mountains were covered with boundless forests of Cypress, Pine, Holm-oak, Maple and other trees, and it is known that Minoan Cretans exported cypress wood to neighbouring countries, chiefly to Egypt.

At that time the island's forests were inhabited by animals which no longer live on the island, such as deer, whose horns have been found in the sanctuary of the Sanke Goddess. It is even possible that wild boars and wild sheep lived in Crete then. Many helmets made of boars' teeth have been found in tombs of the Late Minoan period, while there is evidence that wild sheep continued to live in the Cretan mountains as late as the Venetian era.

The mountains of Crete were still forest-covered during the classical age of antiquity. Characteristic is the fact that the Ida Mountains, or Psiloritis, completely bare today, took their name from the Dorian Ida - forest, woods, forested mountain. Herodotus calls Crete "Hori ipsili te ke idisi sinirefi", that is, covered with trees whose shade is deep.

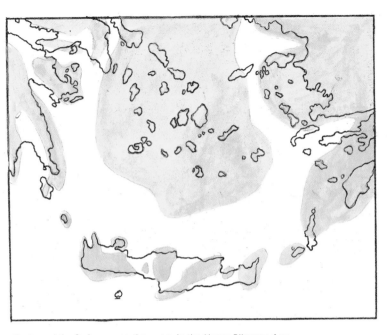

Crete and the S. Aegean as they were in the Upper Pliocene Age.

VENETIAN AND TURKISH OCCUPATIONS

The greater part of Crete's forests were still untouched during the Venetian occupation (1206-1669), as we are able to ascertain from the many European travellers who passed through the island, usually on their way to the Holy Lands.

The Frenchman Jean Palerne, who passed through Crete in 1518, describes the cypress forests surrounding Candia (Heraklion). Henri Castella writes in 1600 that Crete is the happiest island in the Mediterranean - fertile, with a mild climate and all its mountains covered with cypress trees.

In the island's forests at that time there lived a multitude of wild mammals and birds. The Cretan wild goat (Capra aegagrus - cretica) was abundant when Belon passed through in 1554; moreover, at that time there were still wild sheep living on the island although it is not known when they disappeared.

Andre Thevet, who passed through Crete in 1549, notes that birds of prey were abundant on the island. They were hunted and killed for their feathers, used in making arrows, as well as for their skins, which were tanned.

The rapid deterioration of the Cretan environment seems to have started only after the Turkish occupation of 1660. The reasons for this situation, expressed mainly in the strip-

A tuskless pygmy elephant, a Cretan denizen during the Plistocene period.

ping of the mountains' ancient forests, are not documented. We can assume, however, without falling too short of the mark, that the main reasons were the resettlement of a large part of the island's population in the mountainous areas for greater security, the sharp increase in the number of domestic animals allowed to graze in the forests, and the indifference of the Turkish authorities towards their preservation.

Despite all this, as long as men still hunted with bow and arrow or with primitive guns, the populations of mammals and birds were still not severly affected. Tournefort wrote in 1717 that the wild goats lived in herds and Savary noted that the island's high mountains were inhabited only by wild goats.

THE ISLAND'S ENVIRONMENT TODAY

The present-day environment of Crete is strikingly different from that of antiquity, or even that of the Venetian period. The main feature of the Cretan landscape is its bareness: forest-covered land has fallen to less than 10% of the island's total area. This unnatural situation has caused many species of plants and animals to vanish from Crete during the 20th century, while many other species have been driven to the brink of disappearance, or have not been sighted for the past 30 years.

The losses to Cretan nature would certainly be even greater were it not for the island's many gorges, which offer refuge to a multitude of mammals, birds and plants. In spite of its deterioration, however, the Cretan environment remains one of the richest in the Mediterranean region in terms of numbers of species.

THE CLIMATE

The climate of Crete is in general Mediterranean, with long, dry summers and mild winters, accompanied by frequent rains. On the south coast the climate is warmer than on the north coast, while it rains more frequently in western Crete than in the eastern part of the island

In the coastal and plans zones, snow is an extremely rare phenomenon, even in the coldest winters. In the semi-mountainous zone, the summers are dry and extended and the winters mild with frequent rainfall. Snow falls only on the coldest days in the heart of winter, and does not form a permanent cover.

In the mountainous zone the climate is cool in the summer and relatively cold in the winter. In the summer months the days are hot when it is not cloudy, and the nights cool. In winter it rains often, and more rearely snows, especially during the months of January and February, when the snowfall is great enough to form a permanent snow cover. In the highest reaches of the mountainous zone, the snows do not melt until the end of March or even later.

In the sub-alpine zone the winters are more severe and snow covers the grounds from December to April, while in some places it does not melt until the end of May or even later. In summer the days are hot and the nights cold, while rain, fog and changes in the weather are not rare phenomena. Finally, in the alpine zone, weather conditions are even harsher. The snow stays on the ground longer, the nights are colder in summer and it rains more frequently in spring, autumn and even in the summer.

We may observe a unique type of climate in the gorges of Crete. Protection from winds, the relative paucity of sunlight and the somewhat higher atmospheric humidity give the gorges a climate all their own. In summer, for example, they offer a cool refuge for many species of animals and plants, while in winter their climate is wetter than that of the surrounding area.

HABITATS

The Cretan environment is characterised by a wide variety of habitats, relative to height above sea level, proximity to the sea, latitude and longitude, etc. The many gorges form a particular type of habitat, descending as they do from the high mountains and ending usually somewhere near the sea. Another type of habitat can be found in the island's few wetlands.

The coastal zone has its own characteristic flora, made up of plants which have become accustomed to the effect of saltwater. Such plants are Crithmum maritimum, Malkholmia flexuosa, Otanthus maritimus, Calystegia soldanella, Anthemis rigida and many more.

The rocks of the coastal zone, particularly on remote coasts or on Crete's neighbouring

A S.W. Crete coastal habitat.

uninhabited islands, are nesting-places for various seabirds, such as Gulls and Shags. On the same rocks we find colonies of a rare species of bird of prey, the Eleonora's Falcon (Falco eleonorae). In winter other seabirds, such as the Black-headed Gull (Larus ridibundus), the Common Gull (Larus canus) and the Lesser Black-back (Larus fuscus) come down from more northern regions to congregate on the island's coasts.

On the small islands and remote points of N.E. Crete, where there are suitable caves for hiding-places, live a limited number of Monk seals (Monachus monachus). In the past, sea turtles used to come out onto the sandy beaches to lay their eggs, but they no longer lay in Crete.

The plains zone begins at the point where the coastal zone ends and is made up of plains, low hills and foothills of the mountains, up to an altitude of 300 m. above sea level. Even though this zone is mostly cultivated, mechanised farming and pesticides have not wiped out the natural vegetation everywhere. It consists of bushes, such as the oak (Quercus coccifera), the Terebinth (Pistacia terebinthus), the Lentisk (Pistacia lentiscus), the Phoenician juniper (Juniperus phoenicea) or of brush, such as Thyme (Thymus capitatus), or Euphorbia acanthothamnos or Thymelaea hirsuta and various species of Cistus.

A characteristic habitat of the lowland zone, in a region which has not been seriously disturbed by human activities.

In the plains zone we find Hedgehogs, bats, various species of rodents, Badgers, Weasels, owls (Athene noctua) and many species of small birds, which are either permanent residents of the lowlands, summer visitors from africa, or winter visitors which come down from the high mountains. More rarely one may see hares, martens, partridges and Quail, which were abundant in the past but / whose populations have now been decimated.

The semi-mountainous zone begins at about 300 m. and extends up to about 800 m. above sea level. It is pre-eminently a region of shrubs, such as Holm-oak, Kerm oak, (Arbutus unedo) Strawberry-tree, / Greek strawberry-tree (Arbutus adrachne), the various species of Phlomis, Cistus, etc. Many bulbose plants also grow here, such as Urginear Maritima, the Asphodel, various species of cyclamen, Wild onions (allium), Tulipa saxatilis, Asphodeline lutea, and Iris inguicularis - cretensis.

In the semi-mountainous zone live hares, Badgers, Weasels, martens, Hedgehogs, Rooks, crows, Blackbirds, Chukars (Alectoris chukar), Kestrels (Falco innunculus), various rodents, bats and many species of small birds.

In the mountainous zone, ranging from altitudes of 800 m. up to approx. 1800 m., the island's large plateaus, such as the Omalos, Nida and Lassithi, must be included. The mountainous zone was once predominantly forest, but today it has been denuded for the

A characteristic sub-montane region in E. Crete.

most part. Where forests still exist, they are usually made up of Calabrian pine (Pinus brutia) and Italian cypress (Cupressus sempervirens) and very rarely of century-old Hold oak. Predominant in unforested areas are thorny brush, bare rock and which hang down over the steep mountainsides.

The mountainous zone is the natural habitat of many of Crete's burds of prey, such as the Bearded Vulture, the Golden Bagle, the Griffon Vulture, the Lanner Falcon (Falco biarmicusfeldeggii), the Buzzard (Buteo buteo), and the Bonelli's Eagle (Hieraeetus Fasciatus), among others. Here we may also observe many smaller birds, permanent residents or migrants, such as the Jay (Garrulus glandarius), the wookpigeon (Columba palumbus), the Chaffinch (Fringilla coelebs), the Blue Tit (Parus caeruleus), the Sardinian Warbler (Sylvia melanocephala), the Blue Rock Thrush (Monticola solitarius), the Black-eared Wheatear (Oenante hispanica), the Stonechat (Saxicola torquata), the Alpine Swift (Apus melba), and others. The most conspicuous mammal of the mountainous zone is the Cretan wild goat, which now inhabits only the White Mountains. Other mammals include the Cretan marten, the Cretan wild cat, the Cairor spiny mouse, the Edible Dormouse, the Hare, and various other small mammals, both rodents and bats.

Between altitudes of 1800 m. and 2200 m. above sea level stretches the sub-alpine zone, which constitutes a distinct type of habitat. Here we find bare, stony or rocky ground, where water is scarce or non-existent during the summer. These areas have a very interesting flora, because of the great number of endemic plants; the fauna, however, is limited to large birds of prey, wild goats, which climb to such heights only in summer, and birds which like to live on mountaintops, such as Alpine Swifts and Choughs.

At heights of over 2200 m. one finds the so-called alpine zone, which however is very small

A montane zone view in E. Crete. The slopes of Mt. Dhikti, practically bare of forests, can be seen, also the Lassithi plateau which, like all Cretan plateaux, is cultivated.

in the Cretan mountains, as only two mountains are higher than 2200 m. As a habitat, the alpine zone is not essentially different from the sub-alpine.

The gorges of Crete are especially interesting habitats, full of life and energy.

Aside from the rare plants which grow on their steep sides, gorges are a refuge for many representatives of the animal kingdom, such as martens, Weasels, bats, various rodents, Rock Doves (Columba livia), Crag Martins (Ptynoprogne rupestris), Kestrels (Falco tinnunculus), etc.

Wetlands are another type of habitat of great interest, particularly as regards the preservation of species of migratory birds, which use them as resting-places. Such wetlands are very rare in Crete and with the exception of Kourna Lake, the rest are small bogs or mouths of torrents, limited in area. Twice a year migratory birds stop at these places, on their way from Africa to Europe or vice versa. Some of these are the Glossy Ibis (Plegadis falcinellus), the Ruff and Reeve (Philomachus pugnax), the little Egret (Egretta garzetta), the Great Shipe (Gallinago media), the Collared Pratincole (Glareola pratincola), the Black-winged Stilt (Himantopus himantopus), the Ferruginous Duck (Aythya nyroca), the Great White Egret (Egretta alba), among many others.

Many European birds, driven away by the cold and snow, come to the wetlands of Crete to pass the winter. Among them are the Great Crested Grebe (Podiceps cristatus), the Grey Heron (Ardea cinerea), the Mute Swan (Cygnus olor), the Pintail (Anas acuta) and the Coot (Fulica atra).

THE MAMMALS

Within the area of Crete, on the land and in the surrounding seas, at least 30 species of large and small mammals have been sighted with certainty. We say "at least" because it is possible that in the past few years others have been found whose identity is not yet known to us. In particular, certain species of bats and rodents of worldwide distribution, not mentioned in the following list, may very possibly be present in Crete.

The mammals of Crete usually belong to familiar species of neighbouring countries (Balkans, Middle East, North Africa) but often present certain small differences, which indicate completely local subspecies.

Even though the number of species can be considered quite large, as it includes more than one third of the mammals of the whole of Greece, the populations of some of them are very small or are being reduced rapidly. The Cretan Wild goat, for example, is today preserved in very limited numbers in the White Mountains around the Samaria Gorge. The sole reason it is not threatened with extinction is the fact that it has been introduced to the islets Dias, Thodorou and Agioi Pandes and has bred there. The Monk Seal is now living only on the coasts and islets of NE Crete and the Paximadia Islets of S Crete. The future of the species does not look very rosy and a conservation campaign is under way to save it throughout the Aegean.

The main reasons for the reduction in numbers of so many mammal populations are persecution by man the pollution or destruction of their habitats.

1. Erinaceus concolor (Hedgehog)

A small animal for the order Insectivora. Length 18-25 cm. Body covered with hair and thick, strong spines, up to 20 mm. in length, particularly on the back and sides. Generally grey in colour, face and feet darker. Habitat open land, shrub or brush, fallow or cultivated fields from sea level to the mountainous zone. Bears 2-9 young once or twice a year (May to July and August to September). Feeds on insects, snails, roots, bulbs, fruit, frogs and even carrion. Populations decreasing due to pesticides. Range throughout the island.

2. Crocidura gueldenstaedti (Asian Shrew)

Shrews are small insectivorous mammals, whose bodies are similar to those of mice. Ears short, snout long and pointed. An Asian species, Crocidura gueldenstaedti, has been reported in Crete, although its presence has never been confirmed. There are certainly shrews in Crete, but we are not in a position to know to which species they belong, whether to one or several.

3. Rhinolophus ferrum—equinum (Greater horseshoe bat)

Flying mammal of the order Chiroptera; total length including tail about 10 cm., wingspan up to 38 cm. Nose flattened. Ears relatively small and pointed. Colour grey, wings darker. Feeds on insects caught on the wing during the night. Scattered throughout the island.

Hedgehog.

Greater horseshoe bat.

4. Rhinolophus hipposideros (Lesser horseshoe bat)

Similar to 3 but smaller. Length of body and tail approx. 9 cm. Wingspan up to 22 cm. Underbelly darker than upper parts. Nocturnal, insectivorous. Scattered throughout the island.

5. Rhinolophus blasii (Blasius' horseshoe bat)

Similar to 3 and 4 but fur pale buff and wings brown. Length about 9,5 cm. Somewhat rare, mountainous areas.

6. Eptesicus serotinus (Serotine)

Similar to 3 in size, but colour paler and ears larger. Insectivorous species. Mountainous zone. Somewhat rare.

7. Myotis oxygnathus (Lesser mouse-eared bat)

Similar to 3 but snout more pointed, ears longer and narrower, rounded on the tips. Fur buff, wings darker. Body and tail length up to 12 cm. Wingspan 30-35 cm. Nocturnal, feeds on insects. Many areas of Crete.

8. Miniopterus schreibersii (Schreiber's bat)

Habitat open fields and plains, colour greyish-buff. Snout small. Ears short and wide, rounded at tips. Tail represents half of total length of 10-11 cm. Wingspan about 25 cm. Night-flying insectivore. Scattered throughout the island.

9. Oryctolagus cuniculus - subspecies huxleyi (Cretan wild rabbit)

Well-known mammal of the order Lagomorphia, a relative of the Hare. The wild ancestor of the domesticated Rabbit. Colour generally greyish buff. Length up to 40 cm., weight up to 2 kgs. Ears smaller than Hare's, uniform in colour. Hind legs shorter than Hare's. Tail small, blackish above, whitish below. Breeds often, from 2-8 times a year. Young born naked and blind. Feeds on grass. Usually grazes at night. Lives only on the neighbouring islets of Dias and Thodorou. An endemic subspecies, similar to typical form but smaller.

10. Lepus europaeus or Lepus capensis (Brown hare)

Similar to Rabbit but larger, up to 55 cm. in length and 3 kg. in weight. Ears larger, hind legs longer. Bears 3-4 litters a year, each of 2-4. Young born with eyes open and with a furry coat. Fur rather greyish, belly white, usually white spot on forehead. A vegetarian. Range throughout Crete.

11. Glis glis - subspecies argenteus (Cretan Edible or Cretan Fat)

A rodent, similar to a squirrel, but grey in colour with whitish underparts. Bushy tail not held over the back as in squirrels. Probably breeds once a year. 2-7 young. Feeds on seeds, fruit, tender roots, insects and less often birds' eggs and nestlings. In summer sleeps by day, high in tree, becoming active at night. Hibernates in winter in hollow tree or in cavities in the ground under trees. Body length up to 19 cm., tail up to 15 cm. Endemic Cretan subspecies. Range throughout the island, wherever there are trees, mainly in mountains.

Serotine.

Lesser mouse - eared bat.

Little Brown Hare.

17

12. Apodemus sylvaticus - subspecies creticus (Cretan common field or Cretan wood mouse)

A wild version of the House mouse. Tail long and naked. Ears rounded. Fur dark brownish or greyish-brown, underparts white. Feet pale in colour. Body length 80-85 mm., tail 70-90 mm. Cretan subspecies generally slightly smaller and darker than typical form. Several litters a year of 2-9 young. Feeds on seeds, fruit, green plants, bulbs, mushrooms, insects, etc. Active at night. Less active in winter, but does not hibernate. Bounds like kangaroo, up to 90 cm. high. Lives in underground holes and burrows in fields, open ground, and gardens. Rarely enters houses. Common throughout Crete.

13. Rattus rattus (Black or ship rat)

Large rodent, a menace to man. Tail naked and long. Colour usually blackish, less often brownish black above and grey beneath (subspecies alexandrinus) or brown above and cream-coloured beneath (subspecies frugivorus). Body length 16,5-22,8 cm., tail up to 25 cm. Cosmopolitan species, carried on ships. Inhabits buildings, warehouses, sewers seaports, etc. Five litters of 5-10 young per year. Omnivorous. Range almost everywhere on the island, especially in seaside towns.

14. Rattus norvegicus (Brown or Common rat)

Similar to above, but larger. Body length 20-26 cm., tail 17-23 cm. Weight up to 500 gr. Fur dark brown, underparts lighter. Cosmopolitan species, which migrated from Asia to Europe and was carried all over the world on ships. Omnivorous and extremely destructive to man. Present especially in seaports, warehouses, even cultivated fields. Range throughout Crete, mainly flat country.

15. Mus musculus (House mouse)

Small house rodent, common everywhere. Body length 7-9 cm., tail about same length. Fur brownish grey or grey with slightly paler underparts. Tame white mice sold in cages as pets are albino variety of the House mouse. Breeds up to 10 times per year, with 5-6 young in each litter. Diet quite varied, but basically consists of seeds and grain. Distribution throughout the inhabited world. Lives in all towns and villages on Crete.

16. Acomys minus (Cretan spiny mouse)

Endemic rodent of Crete, an African genus, not present elsewhere in Europe. Fur brownish, underparts white. Among fur on back and sides are spines, like those of Hedgehog. The similar but slightly larger species Acomys cahirinus inhabits Cyprus, Israel, Pakistan and Africa. The Cretan spiny mouse lives in dry rocky terrain and enters houses only during cold winters. Breeds 1-5 times a year. Omnivorous, but prefers grain and other plant food. Body length 8-10 cm., tail slightly longer. Scattered throughout the island, in semi-mountainous zone.

17. Cricetulus migratorius (Grey or Migratory hamster)

Readily discernable from the other rodents of Crete by its short tail. Body length 8.7-11,7 cm. Tail length 2,2-2,8 cm. Colour reddish-brown with paler underparts and feet. Central Asian species, scattered westwards to Bulgaria, the Ukraine and Greece. Feeds on seeds, insects, bulbs, etc. Lives in the countryside, where it constructs burrows with 1-5 tunnels which reach a depth of 1.20 m. Nocturnal. It is not certain whether it hibernates or not. Bears 2-3 litters a year of 5-6 young. Thinly scattered over the whole island.

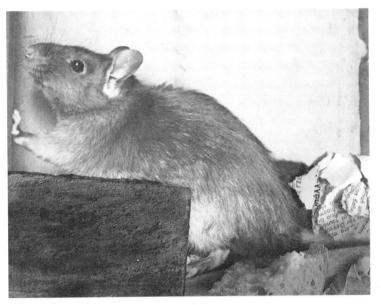

Black or Ship rat.   *House mouse.*

18. Meles meles - subspecies arcalus (Cretan badger)

Mammal of the Mustelidae family, with short legs, relatively long body and short tail. Coat generally silvery white on back, sides and tail. Belly, chest and feet black. Black stripe runs through each eye. Typical form (Meles meles - subspecies meles) has a body length of 75-93 cm. The Cretan subspecies arcalus is generally smaller. Breeds once a year or oftener. Feeds on roots, fruit, beetles and other insects, snails, seeds, etc. Nocturnal. Lives on forest edges, up to 1500 m. Rather common animal in Crete. Cretan common name: Arcalos.

19. Mustela nivalis - subspecies galinthias (Cretan weasel)

A small animal of the Mustelidae family, with short legs, long body and shortish tail, slightly bushy on the tip. Fur dark brown with a greyish-yellow hue, underparts paler. Male is noticeably larger than female (length excluding tail up to 18 cm.). Males have tail of up to 5,5 cm. and females 2,5 cm. Two litters a year of 3-8 young. Lives in forests, rocky country and scrubland and feeds on mice, rabbits, eggs, small birds, frogs, etc. Endemic form common throughout the island. Cretan common names: Kaloyiannoú or Sentakhtári.

20. Martes foina - subspecies bunites (Cretan beech marten)

Similar to the Weasel but much larger: body 45 cm., tail 23-25 cm. long. Colour of typical form is brown or brownish grey, with white chest and throat. In the Cretan subspecies (bunites) the body is dark buff and the legs, tail and muzzle are blackish. Only the throat is white, while the chest is the same colour as the rest of the body. The Cretan marten lives in rocky terrain, sparse woods, scrubland and gorges. Feeds on rodents, worms, bird's eggs, fruit, birds, etc. Raids chicken coops. Present all over the island. The same subspecies lives on Carpathos, the Cyclades and the Sporades. Cretan common name: Zourida.

21. Felis sylvestris - subspecies agrius (Cretan wild cat)

Endemic form of the widespread European wild cat. The only wild member of the cat family on Crete. Body length up to 50 cm., tail up to 30 cm. in males. Females smaller. Tail narrow at the base, becoming bushy on the end. Fur generally light in colour, with dark spots and bars. There are a few black rings on the tail, whose tip is always black. Usually lives in wooded areas and rocky mountainsides. Feeds on hares, birds, insects, rodents, etc. Breeds once or twice a year. Now extremely rare on the island, in danger of extinction, mainly due to the use of poisons (pesticides, rat poison, etc.) out of doors. Cretan common name: Fourógatos

22. Monachus monachus (Monk seal)

The only mammal of the order Pinnipedia living near Crete. Its skin is covered by a short, thick, shiny coat, deep chocolate brown on back and grey underneath. Reaches a length of 2.70 m. and weight of 320 kg. Its hind legs have been reduced to tail flippers, while the foreflippers are small, suitable only for swimming. Gives birth to a single pup, on rocky shores in caves whose entrances are below the waterline. Feeds on fish. Only a few of these animals have been observed on the Paximadia Islands, off southern Crete, on the NE coast of Crete and the surrounding barren islets. An extremely endangered species, threatened with total extinction due to persecution by hunters, destruction of its habitats and pollution of the sea.

Cretan badger.

Cretan beech marten.

23. Capra aegagrus - subspecies cretica (Cretan wild goat)

The pride of Crete's fauna, the local race of the Asian species Caprus aegagrus. After World War II, the misnomer kri-kri has been attached to this animal, but the Cretan people have always called it Agrimi. The male is about 1 m. in length. Colour is at first greyish-brown, but becomes gradually lighter with age until it is completely silvery-white. A black band runs down the middle of the back and another around the neck. The tail is also black, the face dark. The horns of the male are shaped like curved daggers and grow backwards from the head. About halfway along, the horns begin to curve away from each other, but the tips converge and in fully mature adults they meet and cross. This is one of the features of a pure-bred animal, because if there has been interbreeding with domestic goats the tips of the horns curve away from each other. The female is smaller than the male, with much smaller horns and is greyish-brown in colour. The Agrimi lives in rocky terrain at all altitudes and feeds on wild plants. Bears 1-3 young each spring. Its range is now limited to the White Mountains and the Samaria Gorge and it has been introduced to the islets Dias, Thodorou and Agioi Pandes, off northern Crete. It was formerly common throughout the mountains of Crete. In the White Mountains many animals are the products of interbreeding with domestic goats.

24. Turslops truncatus (Bottle-nosed dolphin)

A cetacean with a streamlined body, horizontal caudal fin, short beak and small dorsal fin.

Above: Current distribution of Mediterenean Seal in the Cretan area. Bottom: Current distribution of Cretan Wild Goat.

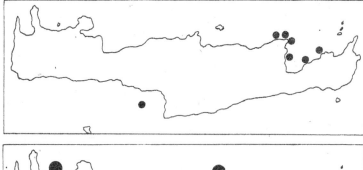

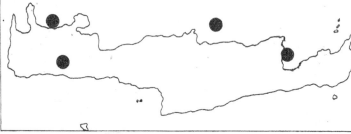

Monk seal.

Cretan wild goat.

Grey in colour. Up to 3,60 m. long. Inhabits the open seas around Crete. Moves in small groups. Feeds on fish.

25. Delphinus delphis (Common dolphin)

Similar to above but smaller (maximum length 2,60 m.) Greyish-black above with yellowish sides, light belly and two white stripes down the sides. Lives in all seas around the island and feeds on fish.

26. Phocaena phocaena (Common porpoise)

Similar to 25, but smaller up to 2 m. in length, with a very short beak. Greyish-black in colour above, almost white underneath. Fairly common in Cretan and Libyan Seas. Lives in small groups.

27. Globicephala melaena (Pilot Whale)

A very large cousin of the dolphins, reaching a length of 8,5 m. Dark grey in colour. Head bulbous, with no beak. Rarely seen in the vicinity of Crete.

28. Orcinus orca (Killer whale)

Another huge dolphin, reaching a length of 9,50 m. Can be distinguished by the large dorsal fin and two-toned body, white underneath and black above. A carnivore which feeds on large fish and seals. Dangerous to man. Was formerly common in the Aegean, but now is rarely seen there or in the seas around Crete.

29. Ziphius cavirostris (Cuvier's beaked or Goose-beaked whale)

A fairly large cetacean, rarely seen in the seas around Crete. It is 8 m. in length, grey in colour and has a long beak.

Goose beaked or Cuvier's beaked.

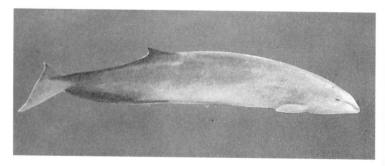

Bottle-nosed dolphin.

Pilot whale.   *Killer whale.*

30. Grampus griseus (Risso's dolphin)

Another rare visitor to the vicinity of Crete. Similar to the Bottlenosed dolphin but larger - up to 4 m. in length. Beak lacking.

THE BIRDS

In contrast to the mammals and other terrestrial animals and plants, the birds of Crete, with only a very few exceptions, scarcely present any variations from their counterparts in other parts of Greece, Europe, Africa or Asia. This is the case because birds can fly over great distances and thus their island populations come into contact with those of neighbouring countries.

In Crete, we find almost all the species of migratory birds which make the trip from Africa to Europe every spring, whether they breed in Crete or are present only during migration. There are also many species which are present the year round, such as the Griffon Vulture, the Bearded Vulture, the Shag, the Chukar, the Rock Dove, the Woodpigeon, the Collared Dove, and the Calandra Lark. These species however are becoming more and more rare, due to hunting, pesticides and destruction of their habitats.

There are also many species which winter in Crete, such as the Coshawk, the Great Grested Grebe, the Grey Heron, the Mute Swan, the Spotted Redshank, and the Mistle Thrush. These species were once much more numerous. Now many of them no longer migrate as far south as Crete, but stop in southern mainland Greece, while others pass through Crete and spend the winter in Egypt.

Although lacking in endemic species, the bird population of Crete is of great interest both as regards the great number of chiefly migratory species which use the island as a stopping-place or spend a good part of the year there, as well as the permanent residents, such as the Bearded Vulture, the Griffon Vulture, etc., which have almost disappeared from the rest of Europe.

Crete is certainly poorer in bird species than it was during World War II or during the 19th century. For example, 25 species of birds recorded during the period 1936-1945 and 5 others recorded in 1852 are no longer present. Among those lost are the Asiatic species Francolinus francolinus (Black Francolin or Black Partridge), noted for its beauty, and Tetrao urogallus (Caperchaillie), both of which were permanent residents on the island.

Family Accipitridae

Diurnal birds of prey, carnivorous, feeding on live animals or carrion, having hooked bills and strong legs with curved talons.

1. Griffon vulture.

2. Griffon vulture (Fot. Tr. Adamakopoulos).

3. and 4. Lammergeyer.

1. Gyps fulvus (Griffon Vulture)

Similar to an eagle, but the head and neck are bare of feathers, covered only by short, thick, white down. The lower legs are bare, the talons smallish and not very curved. The rest of the body is covered in brown feathers. Length 100-110 cm. Wingspan 236-280 cm. Feeds exclusively on carrion, showing preference for the entrails. Nests in small colonies on cliff ledges. Lays only one egg each February. In Crete we find the largest number of Griffon Vultures in Greece and perhaps in the whole of Europe. However, their numbers are being steadily reduced by hunting and poisoned bait laid out by man.

2. Gypaetus barbatus (Lammergeyer)

It and the Griffon Vulture are the largest birds of Crete. The wings are longer and narrower than the Griffon Vulture's. The tail is longer, diamond-shaped. Length 110-150 cm. Wing-

27

span 235-265 cm. In appearance it is something between an eagle and a vulture. Wings, tail and back brownish-black. Head, neck, breast, belly and legs cream or bull to rufous. Immatures almost black with grey underparts. Characteristic of the species are two tufts of long, stiff black "hairs" on either side of the beak. The eyes are reddish. Nests on ledges on sheer mountain-sides. Lays 2 eggs in January. Usually only the stronger chick survives. Feeds on carcasses, particularly the bones, which it swallows whole or breaks by dropping onto a rock from a height. It often follows herds of goats and sheep in lambing season and seizes the placentas. Crete is home to the largest and healthiest population of the species in Europe, which is, however, being steadily reduced.

3. Aegypius monachus (Black Vulture)

A bird similar to the Griffon Vulture but blacker. Its size approaches that of the Bearded Vulture. It feeds exclusively on carrion, on the tough parts of carcasses. Nests in thin forests. Extremely rare.

4. Neophron percnopterus (Egyptian Vulture)

A small vulture, whose size and colour in flight remind one of a Stork. Length approx. 65 cm. Feeds on carcasses, garbage and small animals. In Crete it is present only during migration to and from Africa.

5. Aquila chrysaetos - (Golden Eagle)

Plumage dark brown, with lighter feathers on head and nape . Young birds are the same colour but the base of the tail is white, as are the leg feathers and some of the secondaries. The entire leg is covered with feathers. Beak and toes are yellowish. Nests on cliff ledges, building 2 or 3 large nests which it uses in turn. Usually lays 2 eggs late in February. Length up to 95 cm. and wingspan up to 2,27 m. Only a few pair still live on the island. Feeds on small mammals, birds and tortoises, more rarely on carcasses. An endangered subspecies. Cretan common names: Vitsila or Pnigarovitsila.

6. Aquila rapax (Steppe Eagle)

Similar to the Golden Eagle but smaller: length 67-80 cm. Immatures are buff with dark brown wings and tail. Present in Crete only during migration between Africa and Europe.

7. Aquila clanga (Spotted Eagle)

Similar to the Golden Eagle, but only 62-66 cm. in length. Young birds have dark feathers with pale spots. Nests in forests. Present in Crete only during migration.

8. Aquila pomarina (Lesser Spotted Eagle)

The smallest eagle of Crete, with a length of 54-60 cm. Adults uniform brown in colour. Immatures are spotted, but less so than the Spotted Eagle. Transient in Crete.

1. and 2. Black vulture.

3. Egyptian vulture.   *4. Spotted eagle.*

9. Hieraetus pennatus (Booted Eagle)

Similar to 8, but smaller: length 45-54 cm., wingspan 110-132 cm. Adults greyish brown in colour above, whitish or buff underneath with dark spots. Passes through Crete on migration. Often remains as a winter visitor.

10. Hieraetus fasciatus (Bonnelli's Eagle)

Similar to 9, but larger, with a length of 65-75 cm. and wingspan of 150-170 cm. Adult plumage blackish brown above, whitish below, with a characteristic black band at the tip of the tail. Immatures are dark brown above and light brown on the underparts. Nests on rocky ledges and lays two eggs in February. A permanent resident of Crete, which however is becoming rarer and rarer. Feeds mainly on small birds, but also on small mammals and reptiles. Cretan common names: Skarovitsila.

11. Circaetus gallicus (Short-toed Eagle)

Similar to 10, but greyish brown above and whitish below, with or without dark spots. Length 64-72 cm., wingspan 160-180 cm. Present in Crete only during migration.

12. Buteo buteo (Buzzard)

A rather large bird or prey with broad, strong wings. The tarsus is bare, yellowish in colour. Plumage brown above, slightly paler with dense dark spots below. There are, however, lighter colour phases. Length 52-54 cm. Wingspan 118-140 cm. Nests in tall trees in sparsely-wooded areas and hunts in clearings and open country. Feeds on rodents, reptiles and ground birds. Lays 2-3 eggs at the beginning of April. A common bird of prey in Crete. Its populations are being reduced by hunting and poisons.

13. Buteo rufinus (Long-legged Buzzard)

Similar to 11 but slightly larger and generally more rufous in colour. Nests on rock ledges and hunts in open, dry country. Feeds on small mammals, reptiles and insects. Rare, a migrant in Crete.

14. Buteo lagopus (Rough-legged Buzzard)

Similar to 11 but a little larger with brownish grey plumage and feathered legs. A bird of N. Europe, which migrates southward towards Greece in the winter and rarely reaches Crete. Feeds mainly on small mammals.

15. Pernis apivorus (Honey Buzzard)

Similar to other Buzzards, but smaller, about 53 cm. in length. Colour varies widely, but upper parts usually dark brown, head grey and underparts pale with dark spots. Present in Crete during spring and autumn migration.

16. Milvus migrans (Black Kite)

A characteristic bird of prey, of medium size (47-54 cm. in length), with a somewhat forked tail. Plumage mainly brown, more rufous on the breast and paler on the head. Feeds on small animals, carcasses, insects, garbage, etc. Passes through Crete on migration. Populations steadily declining.

17. Accipiter gentilis (Goshawk)

Similar to 15 but greyish brown, almost black above and white with small dense dark spots below. It has a characteristic white band on the head, above the eyes. Immatures lighter in colour. Length 49-61 cm. Wingspan 100-120 cm. Lays 3-4 eggs in April Nests in trees in thick woods. Feeds on birds and small mammals. A winter visitor to the western half of Crete. Breeds in northern and central Greece.

18. Accipiter nisus (Sparrowhawk)

Similar to 16, but smaller (length 31-38 cm. and wingspan 60-80 cm.). Males smaller than females, more rufous on the breast and behind the eyes. Lays 3-6 eggs in early spring. Nests in trees. May be observed in sparse woods and clearings. Feeds on small birds, insects, more rarely on small mammals. Chiefly a winter visitor to Crete.

1. Lesser spotted eagle Immature.

2. Buzzard (Fot. Tr. Adamakópoulos).

3. Lond-legged buzzard.

4. Black kit.

19. Circus aeruginosus (Marsh Harrier)

Medium-sized bird of prey, with a long narrow tail. Plumage largely brown. In males, tail and part of wings whitish. Nest on the ground in wetland reed-beds and feeds on marsh birds and animals. Length 49-56 cm. Wingspan 116-130 cm. Winter visitor. Populations decreasing.

20. Circus cyaneus (Hen Harrier)

Similar to 19 but smaller (43-50 cm. in length). Females brown with black bands on tail, males grey with black wing-tips. Transient in Crete.

21. Circus macrourus (Pallid Harrier)

Dimorphic species, similar to the Hen-Harrier. Males are grey above and almost white beneath. Females almost identical to the female Hen-Harrier. Passes through Crete on spring and autumn migration.

22. Circus pygargus (Montagu's Harrier)

Dimorphic species. Males resemble Hen-Harrier but underparts are white with vertical rufous stripes. Females almost identical to the female Hen-Harrier. Passes through Crete, especially on spring migration. Only a very few birds have been observed returning to Africa in autumn, when they probably use another route.

Family pandionidae

Diurnal birds of prey which feed always with fishes.

1. Pandion haliaetus (Osprey)

Length 51-58 cm. wingspan 151-158 cm. Colour dark brown above and white at head and under-parts. Nests on trees. In Crete only in passage.

Family Falconidae

Diurnal birds of prey which feed only on prey taken alive.

1. Falco peregrinus - subspecies brookei (Peregrine Falcon)

The best-known of the falcons, widespread throughout the world. The subspecies brookei lives in Crete as well as in the rest of Greece. Length 38-50 cm. Wingspan 113 cm. Plumage dark grey, almost black on the wings and back, buff with small, dense, dark spots on belly, breast and leg feathers. Wings narrow. Nests on rock ledges. Feeds on birds which it catches on the wing. Can reach a speed of 400 kph in a vertical dive. Lays 3-4 eggs in mid-March. Once common, now endangered due to insectisides and illegal hunting.

2. Falco biarmicus - subspecies feldeggii (Lanner Falcon)

Similar to 1 but smaller (28-36 cm.) and browner and more rufous in colour. A very rare species of falcon, a permanent resident in Crete. Endangered species.

3. Falco eleonorae (Eleonora's Falcon)

Similar to 1 and 2 put plumage generally much darker. Some individuals are almost black, while others are more of a dark brown colour. Lives in groups on rocky coasts and the small islands around Crete. Can more rarely be seen inland. Nests on steep cliff ledges. Lays 2-3 eggs at the beginning of August. Leaves for Africa in winter. Feeds on insects, small reptiles and mammals, and also on migrating birds in autumn and spring.

1. *Goshawk.*

2. *Marsh harrier.*

3. *Pallid harrier.*

4. *Osprey.*

4. Falco subbuteo (Hobby)

Similar to Lanner Falcon in colour and size, but plumage on breast and legs more rufous. Transient.

5. Falco columbarius - subspecies aesalon (Merlin)

Length 28-34 cm., wingspan 56-69 cm. Females reddish-brown on the back, buff with dark streaks on breast. Males grey above. Transient in Crete.

6. Falco vespertinus (Red-footed Falcon)

Small falcon, markedly dimorphic. Males greyish-black, with red legs. Females have grey upper parts, buff breast and light rufous head. Transient.

7. Falco naumanni (Lesser Kestrel)

Small falcon (26-33 cm. in length) which lives in colonies in cities and towns, in old houses, where it finds holes suitable for nesting. Lays 4-5 eggs in late April. Females brown with dark spots; males have grey head, brown back and buff breast with dark spots. Feeds on large insects, rodents, lizards, frogs, etc. Summer resident, whose populations are declining, as more and more old houses are being torn down.

8. Falco tinnunculus (Kestrel)

Similar to 7 but slightly larger (length 31-38 cm.). Males have spotted chestnut mantle. Nests on rock ledges and lays 4-5 eggs in late March. Feeds on rodents, reptiles, insects and small birds. A permanent resudent on the island. Becoming steadily rarer.

Family Strigidae

Nocturnal birds of prey.

1. Asio otus (Long-eared Owl)

A medium-sized owl with a length of 35-39 cm. and a wingspan of 85-100 cm. Plumage buff or greyish buff with dark streaks. Belly lighter in colour. Distinguished by its long ear-tufts. Eyes yellow. Habitat forests, clumps of trees, olive groves. Feeds chiefly on small forest-dwelling mammals, which it hunts at night. Lays 4-7 eggs in April in old nest of other bird.

2. Otus scops (Scops owl)

A small owl (20-21 cm. in length). Plumage greyish brown or grey with many dark and white spots. Has short ear-tufts. Lays 3-5 eggs in late April. Feeds on small rodents, insects, small birds, lizards, worms. Nests in holes in trees or walls. Lays 3-6 eggs in April. Habitat olive groves, sparse woods, gardens, ruins. A permanent resident of the island. Very beneficial to farmers.

2. Otus scops (Scops owl)

A small owl (20-21 cm. in length). Plumage greyish brown or grey with many dark and white spots. Has short ear-tufts. Lays 3-5 eggs in late April. Feeds on small rodents, insects, small birds, lizards, worms. Nests in holes in trees or walls. Lays 3-6 eggs in April. Habitat olive groves, sparse woods, gardens, ruins. A permanent resident of the island. Very beneficial to farmers.

Family Tytonidae

Nocturnal birds of prey, similar to the Strigidae.

1. Eleonora's falcon.

2. Hobby.

3. Kestrel.

4. Long-eared owl.

1. Tyto alba (Barn Owl)

The most beautiful owl of Crete. Its colour is greyish chestnut on the back and head with black and white spots. Breast and face are white. In the race guttata, the breast is golden with fewer spots. Nests in ruins, barns, etc. Lays 4-7 eggs in April. May lay for a second time in early summer. Feeds on rodents, reptiles, birds, frogs. Rare in Crete.

Family Caprimulgidae

Nocturnal insectivorous birds with a small bill and feet.

1. Caprimulgus europaeus (Nightjar)

Greyish brown in colour, indistinguishable from the ground or a tree branch. Tail long and narrow. Call insistent and piercing, heard at night. Migratory species. Summer redsident in Crete. Winters in Africa. Migrates by night.

Family Podicepidae

Aquatic birds with sharp narrow bills. Neck rather long. Head with or without crest. Lobed toes help in swimming.

1. Podiceps cristatus (Great Crested Grebe)

Plumage grey above, almost white on neck, breast and belly. A double crest on the crown of the head and feathery projections on the sides towards the back. This plumage, however, is almost always lost in winter. Length 45 cm. Lakes and marshes. Winter visitor.

2. Podiceps nigricollis (Black-necked Grebe)

Similar to 1 but smaller, about 30 cm. long. In summer the back, neck and head are almost black. Light-coloured crest. In winter almost identical to 1 in colour. Lakes and marshed. Transient.

3. Tachybaptus ruficollis (Little Grebe)

Smaller than 1 or 2 (25 cm. long.) In summer upperparts dark, underparts grey. Neck rufous. Head almost uncrested, black on crown. Winter plumage is the same as that of 1 or 2. Lakes and marshes. Winter visitor.

Family Procellariidae

Long-winged seabirds which glide over the surface of the water for great distances. Webbed feet.

1. Calonectris diomedea (Cory's Shearwater)

The entire upper part of the body is grey, the lower part shows all white when in flight. The bill is elongated, slightly curved at the tip. Length 48 cm. Wingspan 110 cm. Open seas around Crete. In spring it nests on sea cliffs and uninhabited islands.

2. Puffinus puffinus (Manx Shearwater)

Similar to 1 but smaller, with a length of 35 cm. and wingspan of 80 cm. Darker, almost black, above. Habitat same as that of 1.

Family Phalacrocoracidae

Aquatic birds, generally black in colour. Webbed feet. Elongated bill, slightly hooked at the tip, suitable for catching fish. The Phalacrocoracidae are excellent swimmers and can dive deep into the water. They often swim underwater with only the head protruding.

1. Phalacrocorax carbo (Cormorant)

Plumage black except for a white band under the base of the bill. Length 90 cm. Winter vi-

1. Scops owl.

2. Barn owl.

3. Great Crested Grebe.

4. Cory's shearwater.

sitor. Fishes in lakes, river deltas, etc. and nests in trees.

2. Phalacrocorax aristotelis (Shag)

Similar to 1 but smaller (about 76 cm.) and completely black. Fishes near shores. Nests on inaccessible rocks and uninhabited islands. Permanent resident of the area.

3. Phlacrocorax pygmaeus (Pygmy Cormorant)

Similar to 1 and 2 but only 48 cm. in length. Black, with white under the bill only. Lives in fresh water and nests in reed-beds and trees. Rare, winter visitor.

Family Pelecanidae

Large aquatic birds, generally white in colour, with short legs, webbed feet, long bill equipped with a pouch underneath for holding the fish on which they feed.

1. Pelecanus crispus (Dalmatian Pelican)

Head/bill length 160-180 cm. Wingspan about 250 cm. Plumage white tinged silver on the back. Legs grey. Pouch orange. Lakes and coasts. Transient in Crete.

Family Ardeidae

Rather long-necked birds with long sharp bills and long thin legs. They inhabit wetlands and walk through shallow water searching for food. In flight they hold the neck retracted into an S-shape.

1. Ardea cinerea (Grey Heron)

The Grey Heron has a long white neck and yellow bill. Breast and belly are white. The back is grey. The characteristic black eye-bands extend backward from each eye into two black ribbon-like feathers which hang free. Length 90 cm. Lives in marshy land and around lakes. Winters in Crete.

2. Ardea purpurea (Purple Heron)

Similar to 1 but neck, breast and belly are rufous. Length about 78 cm. Habits similar to those of 1. Rare transient, present only during migrations between Africa and Europe.

3. Egretta alba (Great White Heron)

Similar to 1 and 2 but pure-white, with black bill and legs. During breeding season the base of the bill and the upper legs become yellow and a bunch of long plumes appear on the back. Length 90 cm. Rare transient.

4. Egretta garzetta (Little Egret)

Almost identical to 3 but toes are yellow and length only 56 cm. A fairly common transient.

5. Ardeola ralloides (Squacco Heron)

Neck relatively short. Plumage buff on back, neck and head, white on belly and under-wings. Legs greenish. A crest of long, ribbon-like decorative feathers on the head. Length 46 cm. Frequently observed, especially during winter.

6. Ixobrychus minutus (Little Bittern)

Similar to 5 but smaller, all buff except for back, wingtips and crown, which are black (brown in immatures). Length 35 cm. Quite common transient.

1. *Cormorant.*

2. *Dalmatian pelican.*

3. *Grey heron.*

4. *Night heron.*

7. Botaurus stallaris (Bittern)

A larger version of 5. Plumage buff with dark spots and crown black. Length 76 cm. A winter visitor or transient. Rare.

8. Nycticorac nycticorax (Night Heron)

Young birds similar to the Bittern but adults have greyish black crown and back, grey wings and white belly, breast and neck. Length 61 cm. Common transient.

Family Ciconiidae

The Ciconiidae are similar to herons in appearance but, unlike herons, they fly with the neck outstretched.

1. Ciconia ciconia (White Stork)

Body white, wings black and white. Bill and legs orange. Length 102 cm. Now only a rare transient in Crete.

2. Ciconia nigra (Black Stork)

Similar to 1 but wings, back, neck and head black. Length 97 cm. Very rare transient.

Family Threskiornidae

Birds similar to herons and storks but with a rather curved bill. Neck outstretched during flight.

1. Plegadis falcinellus (Glossy Ibis)

Plumage brownish red. Long bill, grey legs. Length 56 cm. Transient.

Family Anatidae

Aquatic birds with a somewhat long neck and short legs. Webbed feet. Bill short, flattened on the tip and thick at the base. Males often multi-coloured. Females more uniform in colour.

1. Cygnus olor (Mute Swan)

Large long-necked bird. Bill orange, black at base, with a knob in front of the eyes. Immatures ash-brown. Length 152 cm. Winter visitor.

2. Anas platyrhynchos (Mallard)

The Mallard resembles the tame duck, and is in fact its ancestor. Drake has grey body, green head and neck and rufous breast. Two tailfeathers curl upwards. Duck plainer, greyish brown with darker spots. Length 58 cm. Formerly commoner. Today only a rare winter visitor.

3. Anas quirquedula (Garganey)

Similar to 2 but smaller (38 cm.). Drake has grey body, brown head, greenish on the sides, white throat and black tail, with a vertical yellow band. Duck plain, greyish buff with darker spots. Quite common transient or summer resident.

1. White stork.

2. Black stork.

3. Mut swan.

4. Mallard.

4. Anas crecca (Teal)

Similar to 3 but smaller, about 35 cm. in length. Drake's head has a broad green stripe bordered in yellow. Winter visitor.

5. Anas acuta (Pintail)

Similar in size to the Mallard. Duck resembles duck Mallard. Drake has two long narrow central tailfeathers. Head brown. Body grey above, white below. Neck somewhat longer than other ducks'. Rare winter visitor.

6. Anas nyroca or Aythya nyroca (Ferruginous Duck)

Small duck, 41 cm. long. Drake is chestnut brown, brownish black on back. Duck is greyish brown or greyish black. May once have been a permanent resident of the island. Now only transient.

Family Phasianidae

Birds with short stocky bodies, short triangular bills and short wings. In many species the males are multicoloured (sexual dimorphism). Almost all species nest on the ground.

1. Alectoris chuckar (Chukar)

A short dumpy bird with a short tail. Legs and bill red. Back grey. Belly buff with vertical black flank-bars. Breast and throat white to buff with a black border which starts behind the eyes. Sexes almost identical. Length 33 cm. Nests in rocky country and scrubland. Was once very common in the mountainous and semi-mountainous zones. Rare today, due to unrestricted hunting.

2. Coturnix coturnix (Quail)

Looks like a small partridge, but without the partridge's striking colours. Plumage greyish buff with darker spots. Males have a black throat and a dark necklare-shaped mark just below. Length 18 cm. Inhabits fields in the plains and semi-mountainous zones. Once commo, it is now rare, due to extensive hunting, mechanised farming and pesticides.

Family Rallidae

Birds inhabiting water margins. They have short tails, small sharp bills, rather long legs and long toes, which sometimes flatten out into fleshy lobes.

1. Rallus aquaticus (Water Rail)

Similar to the Woodcock, but smaller (28 cm.). Plumage grey with black bars on flank, wings and back. Bill quite long. Lives in marshes. Rather rare today.

2. Porzana porzana (Spotted Crake)

Similar to 1 but more densely spotted and smaller (23 cm.), with a short bill. Winter visitor.

3. Porzana parva (Little Crake)

Similar to 1 but only 19 cm. in length. Bill short. Pale bars on flanks. Rare transient.

4. Porzana pusilla (Baillon's Crake)

Similar to 1 but bill short and length only 18 cm. Rare transient.

5. Fulica atra (Coot)

Body black. The thick grey legs have fleshy lobes on the toes. Bill white, extending into a white forehead. Length 38 cm. Winter visitor.

1. Pintail.

2. Chukar. (Phot. T. Adamakopoulos).

3. Water rail.

4. Coot.

6. Gallinula chloropus (Moorhen)

Similar to 5 but smaller, with some white on the tail and along the flanks. Legs green. Toes not lobed. Bill red with a green tip. Formerly common, the Moorhen has now almost disappeared from Crete.

Family Gruidae

Large birds, similar to storks but with relatively short bills.

1. Grus grus (Crane)

Colour grey, except for the head and neck, which are black and white. Red crown. Length 114 cm. Transient.

Family Recurvirostridae

Birds with long (often very long) legs and long slender, sometimes upcurved bills. Inhabit marshes.

1. Himantopus himantopus (Black-winged Stilt)

A bird distinguished by its very long, thin, reddish legs. Bill long and straight. Body white, except for wings and back, which are almost black. Rare transient.

Family Burhinidae

Birds of the desert and open plains. Medium-sized bill. Legs quite long, with only three toes. Tail short. Eyes large and staring.

1. Burhinus oedicnemus (Stone Curlew)

Generally sand-coloured, with dark spots. Legs and bill yellow. Length 41 cm. Rare in Crete.

Family Glareolidae

Birds with slender legs, tail usually forked, long wings and small bills. They usually live close to marshes.

1. Glareola pratincola (Collared pratincole)

Plumage greyish brown above and light buff below, turning to white on the belly. Underwings chestnut. Black forked tail. Length 25 cm. Quite common transient.

2. Glareola nordmanni (Black-winged Pratincole)

Similar to 1 but underwings black. Length 25 cm. Rare transient.

Family Charadriidae

Wetland birds with short slender bills, short tails and slender legs of medium length.

1. Vanellus vanellus (Lapwing)

A beautiful bird, metallic green above and white below. Tail, breast and throat black. Nape and head white. Black crest is made up of ribbon-like upcurving feathers. Length 30 cm. Winter visitor.

2. Charadrius hiaticula (Ringe Plover)

Plumage greying buff above, white underneath. Black necklace on breast. Black eye-band and white spot on forehead. Tail black. Length 19 cm. Winter visitor.

1. Moorhen.

2. Stone curlew.

3. Collared Pratincole.

4. Ringed plover.

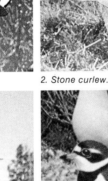

3. Charadrius dubius (Little Ringed Plover)

A smaller version of 2 (15 cm.). Tail is not black, but the same colour as the back. Rare winter visitor.

Family Scolopacidae

Birds with a slender, moderately long or long bill, rarely slightly curved. Legs short of medium length. Tail short. Lives in plains or close to wetlands and in shallow marshes.

1. Scolopax rusticola (Woodcock)

A short squat body, with a large head and long bill. Legs short and muscular. Plumage buff, with dark bars on the underparts. Darker, with black spots on the back and head. Length 34 cm. Winter visitor.

2. Gallinago media (Great Snipe)

Similar to the Woodcock but smaller (28 cm.). Legs dark grey. Head smaller than Woodcock's. Transient.

3. Gallinago gallinago (Snipe)

A smaller version of 1 and 2 (27 cm.), with a longer bill. Winter visitor.

4. Limosa limosa (Black-tailed Godwit)

Looks like a woodcock but the body is slimmer, legs longer and bill more slender and slightly recurved. The breast is grey in winter and rufous in summer. Length 41 cm. Length 41 cm. Winter visitor.

5. Calidris canutus (Knot)

Similar to 4 in colour, but smaller, with a short straight bill. Length 25 cm. Rare winter visitor.

6. Calidris ferruginea (Curlew-Sandpiper)

Similar to 5 but with a longer, slightly curved, bill. Summer plumage rufous-brown, winter plumage grey-buff. Length 19 cm. Rare transient.

7. Calidris alpina (Dunlin)

Similar to 5, but breast greyish-buff with dark spots and bill slightly curved. Length 17-19 cm. Rare winter visitor.

8. Calidris alba (Sanderling)

In summer, grey with dark spots, belly almost white. In winter, plumage lighter-coloured, belly pure white. Bill rather short and straight. Length 20 cm. Rare transient.

9. Calidris temminckii (Temminck's Stint)

A smaller version of 8 (14 cm.), a little darker in colour. Transient.

10. Calidris minuta (Little Stint)

Similar to 8 and 9 but even smaller (13 cm.). Rare transient.

11. Philomachus pugnax (Ruff and Reeve)

Very similar to Calidris. Plumage grey with dark spots. Male (Ruff), unlike female (Reeve), has uniformly grey breast in winter. In summer Ruffs have brighter-coloured plumage and a collar of puffed-out feathers used in mating displays. Length 23 cm. Rare winter visitor.

1. Woodcock.

2. Great snipe.

3. Knot.

4. Sanderling.

12. Numenius phaeopus (Whimbrel)

Similar to Calidris but bill long and curved. Plumage grey with dark spots. Belly almost white. Length 41 cm. Transient.

13. Tringa erythropus (Spotted Redshank)

In summer almost black with light-coloured spots. Winter plumage grey with dark spots, belly white. Bill long and slender. Legs quite long, slender and red. Length 30 cm. Regular winter visitor.

14. Tringa nebularia (Greenshank)

Similar to 13 but with no seasonal colour change. Legs green. Length 30 cm. Regular winter visitor.

15. Tringa totanus (Redshank)

Similar to 13 in winter plumage, but smaller (28 cm.). Winter visitor.

16. Tringa cinerea or Xenus cinereus (Terek Sandpiper)

Similar to 13 in winter plumage, but smaller (23 cm.) with yellow legs and slightly recurved bill. Transient.

17. Tringa stagnatilis (Marsh Sandpiper)

In summer, grey with black spots. In winter, belly white and back grey. Legs and bill grey. Bill straight. Length 23 cm. Winter visitor.

18. Tringa ochropus (Green Sandpiper)

Similar to 17 but colour grey-buff with dark spots and lighter belly. Legs greyish yellow. Length 23 cm. Winter visitor.

19. Tringa glareola (Wood Sandpiper)

A lighter-coloured and smaller version of 18 (20 cm.). Legs yellow. Winter visitor.

20. Actitis hypoleucos (Common Sandpiper)

Very similar to 17 and 18 but whiter on the belly. Length 20 cm. Winter visitor.

21. Arenaria interpres (Turnstone)

A peculiar bird with a short neck, small yellowish legs and a small, slender, grey, slightly recurved bill. Belly white, back greyish brown. Black and white spots on head. In winter colours are more subdued. Length 23 cm. Transient, rare.

Family Laridae

Birds which fly over and swim in the sea, lakes and rivers, but also fly inland. They feed on fish, without shunning garbage, carrion, etc. They usually nest on sea cliffs. Bill of medium length, slightly hooked at the tip. Short legs, webbed feet.

1. Larus argentatus (Herring Gull)

Colour white underneath, grey above. Head white. Bill yellow, legs greyish pink. Tail white. Length 56-66 cm. Common on shores and seas around the island.

1. *Spotted redshank.*

2. *Greenshank.*

3. *Wood sandpiper.*

4. *Common sandpiper.*

2. Larus fuscus (Lesser Black-back)

Similar to 1 but upperparts greyish black and legs yellow. Frequent winter visitor or only transient.

3. Larus audouinii (Audouin's Gull)

Similar to 1 but legs greyish black and bill red, except for the tip which is yellow and is separated from the rest of the bill by a black band. Length 50 cm. Rare Mediterranean species. Lives and nests on the shores of Crete and the nearly rocky islets.

4. Larus canus (Common Gull)

A smaller version of 1 (41 cm.). Legs and bill yellow. Rare transient or winter visitor.

5. Larus melanocephalus (Mediterranean Gull)

Similar to the above species, but legs red. Head almost white in winter and completely black in summer. Wings grey above and white below. Length 39 cm. Winter visitor.

6. Larus ridibundus (Black-headed Gull)

Very similar to 5 but head brownish black in summer and underwings grey, on the tips at least. Length 35-38 cm. Winter visitor.

Family Sternidae

Birds similar to gulls but bill more pointed and tail forked like a swallow's. They inhabit wetlands and usually nest on the ground.

1. Sterna hirundo (Common Tern)

Plumage grey above, white on breast and belly. Tail white. Crown black. Legs red. Bill red with black tip. Length 35 cm. Transient.

2. Sterna sandvicensis (Sandwich Tern)

Similar to 1 but legs and bill black. Length 41 cm. Rare transient.

3. Chlidonias niger (Black Tern)

Similar to 1 but only 24 cm. in length. In summer almost black, in winter greyish white below and dark grey above. Tail not deeply forked. Legs and bill black. Rare transient.

4. Chlidonias hybrida (Whiskered Tern)

Similar to 3 but generally lighter in colour. In summer head whitish with black crown and body dark grey. Legs and bill red. Rare transient.

5. Chlidonias leucopterus (White-winged Black Tern)

Similar to 3, but in summer head, breast and belly black, back and wings grey. Underwings half black, half white. In winter, paler than 3. Legs and bill red. Rare transient.

Family Columbidae

This family contains birds more or less similar to the Domestic Pigeon. They nest in rock crevices or trees. Seed-eaters.

1. Turnstone.

2. Herring gull.

3. Mediterranean gull.

4. Sandwich tern.

1. Columba livia (Rock Dove or Feral Pigeon)

Overall colour grey. Black band on tip of tail. Two black bands on wings. Metallic green hue to neck. White spot on rump. Length 33 cm. Nests on sea cliffs, on rocky islets but also inland, especially in gorges. Formerly common. Today in danger of disappearing due to intensive hunting.

2. Columba oenas (Stock Dove)

Very similar to 1 but lacks black bands on wings and white spot on rump. Size the same. Nests in country with trees. Winter visitor in Crete, where it also lays its eggs in early spring. Seems to move to the north in summer.

3. Columba palumbus (Woodpigeon)

Similar to 1 and 2 but slightly larger (41 cm.). White band on each wing and white patch on the side of the neck. Nests in thick mountain forests. Now a rare permanent resident.

4. Streptopelia decaocto (Collared dove)

Similar to a pigeon but smaller, only 32 cm. long. Colour greyish buff, darker on back. Legs red. Black band on nape. Nests in trees, particularly in towns. Permanent resident but rather rare in Crete.

5. Streptopelia turtur (Turtle Dove)

Similar to 4 but only 27 cm. long. Light brown on back with black spots. Tail black with a white band on tip. Transient. There are however individuals who stay on the island all summer and nest there, in areas with threes.

6. Streptopelia senegalensis (Palm Dove or Laughing Dove)

Similar to 5 but 26 cm. in length. Colour rufous brown on the back and head. Wings greyish black. Belly buff. Tail black with a white edge. A necklace of black spots and lines on the breast. Nests in small clups of trees, especially in palms. Transient in Crete. Has not been reported to nest on the island.

Family Cuculidae

Birds with a long tail and small, slender, slightly curved bill. Most species are parasitic in that they lay their eggs in other bird's nests.

1. Cuculus canorus (Cuckoo)

Colour grey. Tail and wingtips blackish. Belly white, with dense dark bars. There is also a brown phase, which has dark bars not only on the belly but all over the body. Length 33 cm. Summer visitor to the island's mountain forests.

Family Apodidae

Insect-eating birds, similar in appearance to the Swallows. Bill very small. Legs also very small and weak. Wings long and narrow.

1. Apus melba (Alpine Swift)

Overall colour grey with a brownish cast. Throat and rear part of belly white. Tail forked. Length 22 cm. Summer resident. Winters in Africa. Nests on steep mountainsides.

1. Black tern.

2. Rock dove.

3. Stock dove.

4. Wood pigeon.

2. Apus pallidus (Pallid Swift)

A smaller (16,5 cm.) version of 1, but with white throat only. Transient in Crete during migration to and from Africa.

3. Apus apus (Swift)

Similar to 1 and 2 but of a size with the latter. Colour very dark, brownish black with slightly paler throat. Summer resident which nests in buildings in towns and villages. Fairly common.

Family Alcedinidae

Birds with a long sharp bill and short legs. Usually feed on fish, which they catch in their bill, while flying low over the surface of the water.

1. Alcedo atthis (Kingfisher)

A strikingly-coloured bird. Rufous below and blue above. Throat white. Red eye-band. A year-round resident of the island, in wetlands close to the sea. Nests in hole dug in soft cliff face. Rare

Family Meropidae

Insectivorous birds, brightly-coloured. Legs short. Bill slender, pointed and slightly curved. Tail of medium length with two long pointed feathers in the middle.

1. Merops apiaster (Bee-eater)

Breast and belly blue. Crown and back reddish-orange. Tail green. Throat yellow. Black bands on eye and breast. Length 25 cm. A distinctively coloured summer resident. Breeds and nests on the island.

Family Coraciidae

Large multi-coloured birds which feed on small animals. Tail fairly long. Bill short and stout. Short legs.

1. Coracias garrulus (Roller)

Head and underparts blue. Back copper-coloured. Wings and tail bi-coloured, blue and black. Length 31 cm. Summer resident or transient.

Family Upupidae

Birds with a beautiful cresta and a long, slender, slightly curved bill. They feed on insects which they find in rubbish, in manure or rotting leaves.

1. Upupa epops (Hoopoe)

A beautiful bird with brown head, breast and belly. Back, wings and tail barred black and white. Crest feathers brown with black tips. Transient in Crete.

Family Picidae

Birds with a strong bill, which feed on insects which they extract by pecking from the wood of rotting trees or more rarely on insects which they find on the surface of tree trunks. They are able to perch and climb in a vertical position, with two toes pointing forwards, two backwards.

1. Cuckoo.

2. Pallid swift.

3. Swift.

4. Kingfisher.

1. Jynx torquilla (Wryneck)

The smallest member of the family. Because of its small size it does not make holes in wood but eats insects, mainly ants, which it finds on the bark of trees. Overall colour greyish buff with darker spots. Length 16,5 cm. Transient.

Family Alaudidae

Small or medium-sized birds, with or without a crest. Feet adapted to walking on ground, with the rear toe and toenail usually longer than the others. Bill short and conical.

1. Melanocorypha calandra (Calandra Lark)

Plumage grey with dark spots, except for belly and throat which are white. Black necklace on breast. No crest. Rear toenail long. Length 19 cm. Permanent resident of the island.

2. Calandrella brachydactyla (Short-toed Lark)

Similar to 1 but smaller (14 cm.) and lacking black neck-lace on breast. Rear toenail not very long. Summer resident.

3. Galerida cristata (Crested Lark)

Similar to 1 in colour but smaller (17 cm.), with a crest. No black on breast. Rear toenail long. Permanent resident of the island.

4. Lullula arborea (Woodlark)

Bird similar to 3 but slightly smaller (15 cm.) and with a smaller, hardly visible crest. Permanent resident.

5. Alauda arvensis (Skylark)

Similar to 3 and 4 but larger (18 cm.). Crest smaller than that of 3 but more conspicuous than that of 4. Permanent resident.

Family Hirundidae

Long-winged birds with short legs, small bill and forked or unforked tail. Feed on insects, which they catch on the wing.

1. Hirundo rustica (Swallow)

Plumage black above, white below, with reddish-brown throat. Tail deeply forked, with long streamers. Length 19 cm. Common everywhere. Builds its nests in villages and towns. Summer resident.

2. Hirundo daurica (Red-rumped Swallow)

Similar to 1 but tail streamers slightly shorter. Buff on belly extending to throat, nape and rump. Length 18 cm. Builds its nest under overhanging rocks in gorges. Summer resident.

3. Delichon urbica (House Martin)

Similar to 1 but smaller (12,5 cm.) with tail less deeply forked. Underparts and back pure white. Builds its nests on houses and on rocks in gorge walls. Common summer resident.

4. Riparia riparia (Sand Martin)

Similar to 3 but grey, not black, above. Has a grey necklace on breast. Tail small, two-lobed. Length 12 cm. Builds its nest in holes in vertical banks. Summer resident.

1. Bee eater.

2. Roller.

3. Hoopoe.

4. Wryneck.

5. Ptynoprogne rupestris (Crag Martin)

Plumage grey above, very pale greyish buff below. Tail truncated. Length 14,5 cm. Builds its nest below over-hanging rocks. Rare summer resident.

Family Motacilidae

Small or medium-sized birds, with slender, sharp beak, moderately long or long tail and slender legs.

1. Anthus campestris (Tawny Pipit)

Rather large bird (16,5 cm.) with moderately long tail. Colour grey, belly much lighter, wings and tail darker. Lives in mountainous zone. Summer resident.

2. Anthus pratensis (Meadow Pipit)

Similar to 1 but smaller (14,5 cm.) and darker in colour, with dark spots on breast. Winter visitor.

3. Anthus spinoletta (Water Pipit)

In summer it resembles 1, as its breast is uniform buff in colour. In winter plumage however it has spots on its breast, like 2, with which it is easily confused. Length 16,5 cm. Winter visitor.

4. Anthus cervinus (Red-throated Pipit)

Similar to 1 but smaller (14,5 cm.). In summer its breast and throat become rufous, while in winter they are white with black spots. Belly white. Sporadic appearances in winter.

5. Anthus trivialis (Tree Pipit)

Very similar to 2 but overall colour grey, almost buff. Summer resident.

6. Motacilla flava (Blue-headed and Yellow Wagtails)

Relatively small bird, with a long tail. Upper parts of body grey, lower yellow. Tail blackish. Length 16,5 cm. Summer resident.

7. Motacilla cinerea (Grey Wagtail)

Similar in size and colour to 6 but tail longer, almost as long as body, and throat usually black. Permanent resident of the island. Summers in mountains, winters in plains.

8. Motacilla alba (White and Pied Wagtails)

Similar to 6 and 7 but white underneath. Throat black in summer, white in winter. Permanent resident of the island. Winters in plains, summers in mountains.

Family Troglodytidae

Small birds with short rotund bodies, sharp slender bills and short tails, held cocked up.

1. Calandra lark   2. Crested lark   3. Swallow   4. House martin   5. Sand martin   6. Tawny pipit

59

1. Troglodytes troglodytes (Wren)

Colour brown on back, buff underneath, with darker spots and bars, particularly toward the tail. Length 9,5 cm. Year-round resident, common especially in mountains.

Family Prunellidae

Small birds with sharp, slender bills, medium-sized tails, slender legs. They live mainly on mountains.

1. Prunella collaris (Alpine Accentor)

Head, breast and belly grey. Flanks brown-spotted. Back and wings grey, spotted with black. Throat white- and grey-spotted. Tail grey. Length 18 cm. Permanent resident of high mountains.

2. Prunella modularis (Hedgesparrow or Dunnock)

Similar to 1 but darker-coloured. Throat uniform grey. Length 14,5 cm. Winter visitor. Inhabits high mountains.

Family Turdidae

Small or medium-sized birds, with relatively short, slender bills. Legs slender. Tail of medium length.

1. Turdus merula (Blackbird)

Plumage black in male, dark grey in female. Bill yellow, legs grey. Length 25 cm. Once a common bird in Crete, the Blackbird is now becoming rare. Inhabits mountains in summer, descends to plains in winter.

2. Turdus philomelos (Song Thrush)

Plumage greyish brown above, yellowish white with dark spots below. Length 23 cm. Winter visitor.

3. Turdus viscivorus (Mistle Thrush)

Identical to 2 in colour, but larger - about 27 cm. long. Winter visitor.

4. Monticola solitarius (Blue Rock Thrush)

Similar to the Blackbird but males are a dark greyish blue with black wings and tail. Fe-

1. Water pipit   2. Grey wagtail   3. White wagtail   4. Wren   5. Alpine accentor   6. Dunnock

61

males very different: greyish brown, with lighter spots. Length 20 cm. A rare bird in Crete. Probably a permanent resident of the mountainous zone.

5. Monticola saxatilis (Rock Thrush)

Similar to 4 but smaller (19 cm.). Females same as female Blue Rock Thrush but lighter in colour, with brown tail. Male has greyish blue head and back, blackish wings, chestnut tail and belly. Summer resident of mountains.

6. Oenanthe hispanica (Black-eared Wheatear)

Overall colour buff. Wings black. Black wedge-shaped spot over eye. Tail black-tipped, white at base. Rear part of body white. Female identical to male but dark areas brown, not black. Length 14,5 cm. Summer resident.

7. Oenanthe oenanthe (Wheatear)

Similar to 6 but back and crown grey. Length 14,5-15 cm. Summer resident. Inhabits open, bare or sparsely vegetated land.

8. Oenanthe isabellina (Isabelline Wheatear)

Overall colour buff, wings brown. Tail same as that of 6 and 7. Length 14 cm. Rare transient.

9. Saxicola torquata (Stonechat)

Plumage black, except for breast and belly, which are rufous. White streak at base of tail. Female brown, with rufous breast and belly. Length 12,5 cm. Summer resident.

10. Saxicola rubetra (Whinchat)

Back, head and tail greyish brown, with dark spots. Belly, breast and throat buff-rufous. Wings brownish black. Colours same in female, but duller. Length 12,5 cm. Summer resident.

11. Phoenicurus phoenicurus (Redstart)

In male, tail and breast bright chestnut, back and crown grey. Wings greyish brown. Throat and cheeks black. Belly white. In female tail chestnut, rest of body grey-buff, paler below. Length 14 cm. Winter visitor.

12. Phoenicurus ochruros (Black Redstart)

In male, plumage greyish black, belly lighter. Tail chestnut. Female identical, but paler. Length 14 cm. Winter visitor.

1. Blackbird   2. Mistle thrush   3. Blue rock thrush   4. Rock thrush   5. Black-eared wheatear   6. Stonechat

63

13. Luscinia megarhynchos (Nightingale)

Overall colour greyish buff, tail rufous. Length 16,5 cm. This bird, famous for its song, lives and nests in the thick growth of torrent-beds. Summer resident.

14. Erithacus rubecula (Robin)

Plumage greyish brown on upperparts. Belly white, Breast, throat and face rufous. Length 14 cm. Winter visitor.

Family Sylviidae

Small insect-eating birds with slender bills.

1. Sylvia hortensis (Orphean Warbler)

Plumage dark grey above and light grey below. Head black, except for throat. Tail blackish. In female, head grey. Legs blackish. Length 15 cm. Summer resident.

2. Sylvia atricapilla (Blackcap)

Similar to 1 but only crown black in male, brown in female. Length 14 cm. Permanent resident or winter visitor.

3. Sylvia melanocephala (Sardinian Warbler)

Similar to 1 but slightly smaller (13,5 cm.) Back grey but with a slightly more reddish tinge than that of 1. Legs slightly paler. Permanent resident of mountainous and semi-mountainous zones.

4. Sylvia ruppelli (Ruppell's Warbler)

Similar to 1 but male has black throat and white mountachial stripe. Female has dark spots on throat. Length 14 cm. Summer resident.

5. Sylvia conspicillata (Spectacled Warbler)

Similar to 1 but wings greyish brown and belly light greyish buff. Head greyish black. Length 12,5 cm. Summer resident.

6. Sylvia candillans (Sybalpine Warbler)

Similar to Rüppell's Warbler, with the characteristic white moustachial stripe, but throat and breast rufous in male and dark buff in female. Length 12 cm.

7. Sylvia communis (Whitethroat)

Male and female almost identical. Head and back grey. Wings and tail greyish brown. Underparts very pale buff-grey. Length 14 cm. Summer resident.

1. Whinchat   2. Redstart   3. Black redstart   4. Robin   5. Orphean warbler   6. Blackcap

8. Sylvia borin (Garden Warbler)

Very similar to 7 but back and head dark grey and underparts very pale grey. Length 14 cm. Transient.

9. Sylvia sarda (Marmora's Warbler)

Similar to 7 but back dark grey and underparts darker than those of 7. Female slightly paler. Length 12 cm. Summer resident.

10. Hippolais icterina (Icterina Warbler)

Plumage olive green on back and head, light greenish yellow on underparts. Wings and tail dark olive green-black. Characteristic light-coloured stripe, like an eyebrow, above the eye. Length 13,5 cm. Summer resident.

11. Hippolais pallida (Olivaceous Warbler)

Similar to 10 but overall colour more buff. Summer resident.

12. Acrocephalus arundinaceus (Great Reed Warbler)

A wetland bird. Plumage greyish brown on upperparts, pale greyish buff below. Tail rounded. Length 19 cm. Rare summer resident.

13. Acrocephalus scirpaceus (Reed Warbler)

A smaller version of 12 (12,5 cm. long). Inhabits wetlands. Summer resident.

14. Acrocephalus palustris (Marsh Warbler)

Almost identical to 13 but back a little darker. Inhabits wetlands. Transient.

15. Acrocephalus melanopogon (Moustached Warbler)

Plumage buff below, brown with dark streaks above. Throat buff, crown and cheeks dark greyish brown. Pale eyestripe. Length 13 cm. Transient, possible a winter visitor. Wetland dweller.

16. Acrocephalus schoenobaenus (Sedge Warbler)

Similar to 15 but paler. Habitat similar. Transient.

17. Acrocephalus paludicola (Aquatic Warbler)

Similar to 15 and 16 but paler. Pale streak in middle of crown. Transient.

*1. Rüppell's warbler   2. Subalpine warbler   3. Icterine warbler   4. Olivaceous warbler
5. Marsh warbler   6. Aquatic warbler*

18. Locustella luscinioides (Savi's Warlber)

Wetland dweller, plumage dark brown above and buff below. Tail rounded. Summer resident.

19. Cettia cetti (Cetti's Warbler)

Similar to 18 but darker, dark rufous brown or brownish black above. Tail broader than 18's. Wetland bird. Probably a permanent resident of Crete.

20. Cisticola juncidis (Fan-tailed Warbler)

Overall colour buff. Underparts uniform in colour. Upperparts with dark streaks. Broad tail which when seen from below has black and white streaks on tip. Wetland bird, permanent resident in Crete.

21. Phylloscopus sibilatrix (Wood Warbler)

Upperparts olive green. Belly almost white. Breast and throat greenish yellow. Legs pale. Length 12,5 cm. Summer resident.

22. Phylloscopus collybita (Chiffchaff)

Similar to 21 but plumage generally less greenish, more of a greyish colour. Length 11 cm. Winter visitor, often a permanent resident.

23. Regulus regulus (Goldcrest)

Very small bird, plumage olive green above, grey below. Wings and tail blackish. Black line above the eye. Crown orange in male and yellow in female. Length 9 cm. Transient.

24. Regulus ignicapillus (Firecrest)

Similar to 23, but colours brighter. Two parallel black eyestripes. Summer, possibly permanent, resident.

Family Paridae

Small insectivorous birds with small bills and moderately long or long tails.

1. Parus major (Great Tit)

Back yellowish olive green. Belly yellow. Wings grey. Tail greyish black. Head black, except for white cheeks. Throat black extending into narrow black band down middle of breast and belly. Length 14 cm. Permanent resident. Summers in mountains, winters at low elevations.

1. Fan-tailed warbler   2. Goldcrest   3. Great tit   4. Blue tit   5. Pied flycatcher   6. Collared flycatcher

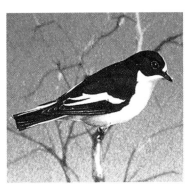

2. Parus caeruleus (Blue Tit)

Similar to 1 but crown greyish blue and black on throat does not extend towards belly. Length 11,5 cm. Permanent resident; summers in mountain forests, winters in plains.

3. Parus ater (Coal Tit)

Similar to 1 but breast and belly buff-grey and length 11,5 cm. Permanent resident, but rather rare.

Sitta neumayer (Rock Nuthatch), a species of the Balkans and Western Asia, has been observed in the past in Crete, but its presence has not been verified recently. It has a strong, sharp bill, short neck, grey back and buff underparts.

Family Muscicapidae

Small birds, with short slender bill and slender legs. They feed on insects caught on the wing.

1. Ficedula (Muscicapa) hypoleuca (Pied Flycatcher)

Sexually bimorphic. Male black above, pure white below. White band on black wings. Female similar but has greyish brown instead of black upperparts and light grey underparts. Length 18 cm. Summer resident.

2. Ficedula (Muscicapa) albicolis (Collared Flycatcher)

Coloration similar to that of 1, especially in female. Male similar, but with white collar and large white spot on forehead. Length 12,5 cm. Summer resident.

3. Muscicapa striata (Spotted Flycatcher)

Overall colour greyish brown, lighter on underparts. Brown streaks on breast. Dark brown streaks on head. Length 14 cm. Summer resident.

Family Certhiidae

Insectivorous birds which creep about tree-trunks. Bill longish, slender and slightly curved.

1. Certhia brachydactyla (Short-toed Treecreeper)

Upperparts dark greyish brown with lighter spots. Underparts pure white. Length 12,5 cm. Permanent resident in forested areas.

Family Oriolidae

Medium-sized birds, usually with bright-coloured plumage. Bill strong, sharp and pointed.

1. Short-toed treecreeper.

2. Golden oriole.

3. Lesser Grey shrike.

4. Red-backed shrike.

1. Oriolus oriolus (Golden Oriole)

Sexes bimorphic. Males are bright yellow all over, except for black wings and tail. Females olive green on back and grey with black spots on breast. Length 24 cm. Transient.

Family Laniidae

Birds of medium size, with long tail, large head, slender legs and strong, thick, relatively short bills, slightly hooked at the tip.

1. Lanius minor (Lesser Grey Shrike)

Plumage grey on back and crown. Underparts very pale grey-buff. Wings and tail black. Broad black eye-band. Length 20 cm. Summer resident.

2. Lanius senator (Woodchat Shrike)

Similar to 2 but crown chestnut-rufous. Length 17 cm. Summer resident.

3. Lanius collurio (Red-backed Shrike)

Similar to 1 but wings and back chestnut. Length 17 cm. Summer resident.

4. Lanius nubicus (Masked Shrike)

Similar to 1 but back and crown black. Length 17 cm. Transient.

Family Corvidae

Large or medium-sized birds, with long or moderately long tails. Plumage brightly-coloured or black. Legs relatively strong. Bills variously shaped.

1. Corvus corax (Raven)

Plumage all black. Legs strong. Bill thick and strong. Length 64 cm. Omnivorous bird, which readily adapts to a variety of environments. Its populations in Crete are still quite large, despite the fact that farmers kill it in the belief that it eats new-born lambs and kids, which is untrue.

2. Corvus corone (Hooded Crow)

Similar to 1 but smaller (47 cm.). Bill more slender. Belly and back grey. An omnivorous bird, common in Crete.

3. Corvus monedula (Jackdaw)

Similar to 1 but smaller (only 33 cm.), with a relatively slender bill. Belly and nape dark grey. Permanent resident of the island.

4. Pyrrhocorax pyrrhocorax (Chough)

An all-black bird, similar to the Raven, but legs reddish and bill red, slender, long and slightly curved. Length 40 cm. Permanent resident of high mountains.

5. Pyrrhocorax graculus (Alpine Chough)

Similar to 4 but bill yellow and noticeably shorter. Permanent resident of high mountains.

6. Garrulus glandarius (Jay)

A beautiful colourful bird. Belly and breast buff. Back greyish brown. Tail black. Flack and white down on crown and a black "mustache" extending backwards from the base of the

1. Masked shrike.

2. Raven.

3. Hooded crow.

4. Chough.

bill. Wings multi-coloured: black, buff, white and metallic blue. Length 34 cm. Rare, permanent resident.

The Magpie (Pica pica) may or may not be present in Crete. Although it may have inhabited the island formerly, it has not been sighted in recent years.

Family Sturnidae

Birds which resemble members of the family Corvidae but are smaller, with a short, straight bill.

1. Sturnus vulgaris (Starling)

Plumage almost black in summer; black with white spots in winter. Legs reddish. Bill greyish yellow. Length 21,5 cm. Winter visitor. Flies in large flocks and feeds on various fruits, olives in particular.

Family Passeridae

Small birds with short conical bills. Mainly seed-eaters.

1. Passer domesticus - subspecies itallae (Italian House Sparrow)

Plumage greyish brown with darker spots on upperparts, grey-white on underparts. Breast and throat blackish. Crown grey, nape brown. Female lacks black on breast and throat and grey on crown. Length 14,5 cm. Common permanent resident in towns, villages and fields.

2. Passer hispaniolensis (Spanish Sparrow)

Similar to 1 but male has brown crown and more black on breast with black spots extending to belly. Length 14,5 cm. Rarer than 1.

3. Passer petronia or Petronia petronia (Rock sparrow)

Similar to 1 but sexes almost alike, having no black on throat or breast. Crown and nape light grey. Male has yellow streak on breast. Length 14 cm. Transient in Crete during migration.

Family Fringillidae

Birds similar to the Passeridae, whose anatomical differences are hard to distinguish.

1. Fringilla coelebs (Chaffinch)

Male has brownish breast, belly and head. Crown grey. Tail greyish black. Wings greyish black with two characteristic white bands close to their base. Female identical on wings and tail, but rest of body is uniform grey-buff. Length 15 cm. Permanent resident. Winters in plains, summers in mountains. Formerly common, is now becoming rarer and rarer.

2. Fringilla montifringilla (Brambling)

Similar to 1 on wings and tail. Head and back black. Breast buff-brown. Belly white. Female similar, but head and back greyish brown with dark spots. Length 14,5 cm. Transient.

3. Serinus serinus (Serin)

Overall colour yellowish green above, yellowish below. Tail dark olive green. The whole body, except for throat and breast, is covered with dark olive-green spots. Female similar, but colours duller. Length 11,5 cm. Permanent resident of island.

4. Carduelis spinus (Siskin)

Similar to 3 but male less spotted. Crown black. Small black spot on throat. Female almost

1. Jay.

2. Italian house sparrow.

3. Spanish sparrow.

4. Rock sparrow.

identical to female of 3. Length 12 cm. Part of its population resides year-round in Crete. In winter it is probably reinforced by migrants from the north.

5. Carduelis chloris (Greenfinch)

Similar to 3 but 4 but larger (14,5 cm.). Lacks dark spots. Permanent resident.

6. Carduelis carduelis (Goldfinch)

Male and female almost alike. Body buff. Tail black. Wings black and yellow. Face red, cheeks white, crown and nape black. Length 12 cm. Common permanent resident.

7. Carduelis (Acanthis) cannabina (Linnet)

Colour largely brown above, buff below. Head buff. Tail white at base, black on tip.

Breast and crown reddish. Female lacks reddish tinge on breast and head but has dark streaks over most of body. Length 13,5 cm. Permanent resident.

8. Bucanetes or Rhodopechys githaginea (Trumpeter Finch)

Similar to 7 but bill shorter and thicker, reddish in male, yellowish in female. Female lacks dark streaks. Length 12,5 cm. Rare vagrant from Africa.

9. Coccothraustes coccothraustes (Hawfinch)

Plumage resembles that of Chaffinch, but Hawfinch is larger (18 cm.) and has a thicker and stronger bill. Winter visitor or transient.

10. Loxia curvirostra (Crossbill)

A very characteristic bird, with a stocky body and a peculiar bill with crossed mandibles. Male reddish with blackish tail and wings. Female greenish, wings and tail darker. Immatures buff with dark spots; wings and tail brownish black. Length 16,5 cm. Lives in mountain forests and feeds on seeds of conifers which it extracts from cones with its specially adapted bill. Until a recent sighting in the White Mountains/Samaria Gorge by the Italian professor B. Massa, this species was not known to live in Crete.

Family Emberizidae

Birds similar in appearance to the Fringillidae and Passeridae; they differ only in secondary and hard-to-distinguish features.

1. Emberiza melanocephala (Black-headed Bunting)

Male yellow below and brown above. Wings and tail blackish. Head black. Female buff below and greyish brown, with dark spots, above. Length 16,5 cm. Summer resident. W. Asian species.

2. Emberiza citrinella (Yellowhammer)

Similar to 1 but male has yellow head. Length 16,5 cm. Winter visitor.

3. Emberiza cirlus (Cirl Bunting)

Similar to 1 but male is yellowish white on underparts; head multi-coloured: crown grey with spots, head yellow with black eyestripe and black throat. Female identical to female Black-headed Bunting but more spotted. Length 16,5 cm. Permanent resident.

4. Emberiza caesia (Cretzschmar's Bunting)

Belly buff. Back, wings and tail buff with brownish black spots and streaks. Head and

1. *Chaffinch*   2. *Brambling*   3. *Siskin*   4. *Greenfinch*   5. *Goldfinch*   6. *Linnet*

breast grey. Throat buff. Female similar but all buff, paler underneath. Head buff with dark spots. Length 16,5 cm. Summer resident.

5. Emberiza hortulana (Ortolan)

Very similar to 4 but head and breast buff-grey. Female almost identical to male. Length 16,5 cm. Summer resident.

6. Emberiza cia (Rock Bunting)

Similar to 4 and 5 but has three black stripes on each side of head. Female similar with duller colours on head. Length 16,5 cm. Permanent resident.

7. Millaria or Emberiza calandra (Corn Bunting)

Belly and breast buff, with dark spots. Head and back brown with dark spots. Wings and tail brownish black. Length 18 cm. Permanent resident of Crete.

1. Trumpeter finch   2. Hawfinch   3. Black-headed bunting   4. Yellowhammer   5. Cirl bunting   6. Cretzschmar's bunting

Species inhabiting Crete during the period 1936-1945:

Anas clypeata	Shoveler
Anas penelope	Wigeon
Anas strepera	Gadwall
Asio flammeus	Short-eared Owl
Aythya ferina	Pochard
Aythya fuligula	Tufted Duck
Bombycilla garrulus	Waxwing
Cercotrichas galactotes	Rufous Bushchat
Charadrius alexandrinus	Kentish Plover
Gelochelidon nilotica	Gull-billed Tern
Hippolais olivetorum	Olive-tree Warbler
Hoplopterus spinosus	Spur-winged Plover
Hydrobates pelagicus	Storm Petrel
Larus minutus	Little Gull
Marmaronetta angustirostris	Marbled Teal
Mergus merganser	Goosander
Mergus serrator	Red-breasted Merganser
Numenius arquata	Curlew
Parus lugubris	Sombre Tit
Phylloscopus trochilus	Willow Warbler
Pluvialis apricaria	Golden Plover
Pluvialis squatarola	Grey Plover
Sylvia curruca	Lesser Whitethroat
Tadorna tadorna	Shelduck

Species inhabiting Crete at least up to 1852:

Francolinus francolinus	Black Francolin or Black Partridge
Milvus milvus	Red Kite
Platalea leucorodia	Spoonbill
Pyrrhula pyrrhula	Bullfinch
Tetrao urogallus	Capercaillie

Two of the species of birds which have vanished from Crete since after World War II. Left: Shelduch; Right: Shoveler.

A pair of Black francolins as portrayed by Achilleas Dimitropoulos. This species disappeared from Crete last century.

The Capercaillie, one of the largest birds in Europe. Up to the last century it resided in the mountains of Crete. Today it has disappeared not only from Crete but also from the whole of Greece, with the exception of the Rhodope range where a very few pairs still remain. The reason for this is, on the one hand, the destruction of its habitats, and, on the other, the merciless shooting of this species.

THE NATURE OF CRETE IN THE MINOAN ART

The inhabitants of Crete during the Minoan period had, as it is obvious, strongly developed the lone for the nature. How would it be different, since these people lived surrounded by a magnificent natural environment. The densely wooded mountains the beautiful flowers, the nice smelling of cypress and "dictamo" the rich populations of birds and wild mammals which lived then on the island, in addition to the mild climate made Crete being a real paradise. So, it is not at all strange that so many themes represented on the wall paintings and generally in art of the minoan period, are taken from the nature. For instance: There are numerous representations of the Cretan wild goat on engraved stones, vases, sarcophagus and other objects of art. Famous is also the wall painting with partridges (Alectoris chukar) today a vulnerable species for Crete. Wild cats, another vulnerable species today, are represented on a wall painting found at Aghia Triada. (Holly Trinity). Wild flowers, lilies, orchids and crocuses are the main representation of other wall paintings.

In the Palace of Knossos the world-famous inverted columns were made of single trunks of centuries-old cypresses.

Top: A painting of dolphins of the species Delphinus delphis, in the palace at Knossos.
Bottom: Partridges, from the famous mural of Knossos known as the "Caravanserai".

PROTECTED NATURAL AREAS

The most important protected natural area of Crete is the famous gorge of Samaria and the surrounding peaks which consist the National Park of "Lefka Ori" (White Mountains), one of the ten Greek National Parks. It was founded in 1962 covers an area of 4.850 h. and its highest altitude reaches the 2.116 m. In the middle and lower zone of the gorge there are forests of three species of trees. Near the exit and at the deeper places of the gorge dominate the planes (Platanus orientalis). The Calabrian pines (Pinus brutia) follow and reach at an altitude higher than 1.000 m, while the cypress (Cupressus sempervirens) is often found higher than 1.500 m. Although, there are cypresses among pines at very lower altitude.

The cypresses of the gorge, as well as those spontaneously growing all over Crete belong to the genuine wild form of the species (Cupressus sempervirensvar. orizontalis).

Beyond the above, the gorge is well known for growing in it many and rare species of flowers, such as the famous Paeonia clusii, the Origanum dictamus (Dictamo), the Ebenus Cretica, the Symphiantha cretica, the linum caespitosum e.t.c.

An amphibian (Bufo viridis) and five species of reptiles have been remarked in the Samaria gorge. The most remarkable reptile is the famous "Liakoni" (Chalcides ocellatus) which lives near the edge of the gorge neighbouring to the Aghia Roumeli village.

Many species of birds nestle permanently and some others for a part of the year in this area. The most rare of them are the Lammergeier the Golden eagle, the Griffon vulture, the Bonelli's eagle and the Hobby.

The most important mammal of the National Park is the famous Cretan wild goat (Capra aegagrus - cretica) which lives in small groups on the slopes of the gorge. The nowadays very rare Cretan wild cat (Felis silvestris - agrius) called by the inhabitants "Fourogatos", lives here also.

Other mammals of gorge are the Hedgehog, the Brown hare, the Cretan fat, the Cretan spiny mouse, the Cretan weasel, the Cretan badger and the beautiful Cretan marten or "Zouridha" the population of which has increased extremely, are some other mammals of the gorge.

The second area in Crete enjoying some protection of the human activities is the unique palm forest at Vai found in the East end of Crete. It is a valley crossed by a brook flowing in the sea. The ravine is covered with the unique endemic species Phoenix theophrastii. The fauna of the area is not of a special interest.

Some small islands that are found near Crete, as Dhia, Thothorou and Aghii Pantes and where wild goats were brought by men to live on, are also protected. Wild rabbits, an endemic subspecies called Oryctolagus cuniculus - huxleyi live also on these small islands.

PROBLEMS OF ILLUSTRATION

The greatest problem that I had to face in order to complete this book was the illustration. Unfortunately, I had in my hands only a small part of the necessary photographic material mine or borrowed by my friend Triantaphillos Adamakopoulos. To collect photos for covering the needs of such a book would demand plenty of means (telephocus etc.) as well as some years of work in the country. But the necessity of issueing a book for the birds of Crete the soonest possible, made impossible, at least for the present moment, the following of this method.

The case of buying some slides from greek or foreigner ornithologists who take photographs of birds since many years was excluded from the very beginning as the cost of the book should be increased too much and its issue should not be profitable.

A Lammergeier in the Samaria Gorge (Photographed by Tr. Adamopóulos).

Naturally as a painter I could find refuge in the solution of the painting illustration. Although, it would demand work of at least three years, which should be paid, increasing again the cost of the entire issue.

I front of this impasse, I took refuge in the only realizable solution, under these conditions, that means the solution of photomontaz. I cut very carefully pictures of birds and mammals from different books and putting it on a suitable background photograph, looking like their natural environment I photographed it again with slides. I achieved in this way an enough satisfactory result. The most important is that this result cannot be considered to be "robbery" as there is a reformation and a creation of a new photograph.

The 90% of the pictures of this book are result of photomontaz system. The rest of the pictures are real photographs of alive or embalmed mammals and birds. The name of the owner is referred under the photographs that are not mine.

George Sfikas

INDEX OF MAMMALS

Latin names

A Samaria Gorge view.

Crocidura gueldenstaedti 14

Delphinus delphis 24

Eptesicus serotinus 16
Erinaceus concolor 14

Felis silvestris-agrius 20

Glis glis-argenteus 16
Globicephala melaena 24
Grambus griseus 24

Lepus capensis 16
Lepus europaeus 16

Martes foina-bunites 20
Meles meles-arcalus 20
Monachus monachus 20
Mus musculus 18

Mustela nivalis-galinthias 20
Myniopterus schreibersii 16
Myotis oxygnathus 16

Orcinus orca 24
Oryctolagus cuniculus-huxleyi 16

Phocaena phocaena 24

Rattus norvegicus 18
Rattus rattus 18
Rattus rattus-alexandrinus 18
Rattus rattus-frugivorus 18
Rhinolophus blasii 16
Rhinolophus ferrum equinum 14
Rhinolophus hipposideros 16

Tursiops truncatus 22

Ziphius cavirostris 24

INDEX OF MAMMALS

Common names

Asian shrew 14

Black rat 18
Blasius' horseshoe bat 16
Bottle-nosed dolphin 22
Brown hare 16
Brown rat 18

Common dolphin 24
Common porpoise 24
Common rat 18
Cretan 18
Cretan badger 20
Cretan beech marten 20
Cretan common field 18
Cretan edible 16
Cretan fat 16
Cretan spiny mouse 18
Cretan weasel 20
Cretan wild cat 20
Cretan wild goat 22
Cretan wild rabbit 16
Cretan wood mouse 18
Curvier's beaked 26

Goose-beaked whale 24
Greater horseshoe bat 14
Grey hamster 18

Hedgehog 14
House mouse 18

Killer whale 24

Lesser horseshoe bat 16
Lesser mouse-eared bat 16

Migratory hamster 18
Monk seal 22

Pilot whale 24

Rissós dolphin 26

Schreiber's bat 16
Serotine 16
Ship rat 18

A W. Crete view taken in the region of the village of Lakki. The combination of cultivated olive-trees and fields with the indigenous vegetation - Cypresses and plane-trees - is clearly to be seen.

INDEX OF BIRDS
Latin names

INDEX OF BIRDS
Common names

FOREIGN BIBLIOGRAPHY

Bruun B.   Birds of Britain and Europe

Burton M.   Guide to the mammals of Britain and Europe

Barnard Chr.   Guide to the mammals of Britain and Europe

Heinzel H. - Fitter R. - Parslow J. Birds of Britain and Europe with North Africa and
                                     the Middle East

Vallianos C.   Les oiseaux observès en Crète - Biologia Gallo-
                                     Hellenica - Vol. 11. - 1984

GREEK BIBLIOGRAPHY IN THE GREEK LANGUAGE

Gant Tz.   Information for the management of Eleonora's
                                     falcon (Falco eleonore) in S. Aegean sea.

Demetropoulos A.   Popular names of the Greek birds - magazine.
                                     "Taxidevontas" (Travelling).

Demetropoulos A.   The Golden eagle in Greece - Monography of a
                                     species in danger.

Demetropoulos A.   Along with the Eleonora's falcon at the Aegean
                                     islands magazine (Travelling)

Kanellis A - Muller G. Weick F.   Marsh dwellers and aquatic birds of our country.

Kanellis A.   "The Vultures"

Kanellis A.   The names of the mammals of Greece - magazine «Η
                                     φύσης» (The nature) No. 21-1980.

Kanellis A. - Khantzissarantos   The mammals of Greece - 1963.
Kh.

Katsadorakis G.   The fauna of vertebrates of National Park of White
                                     mountains (Samaria) Crete.

Ontrias J.   The fauna of mammals in Greece - 1967.

Sfikas G.   The greek nature through the centuries.

Sfikas G.   The names of the mammals of Greece - 1978.

Hartmout V.   The Eleonora's falcon (Falco eleonore) in Greece.

Khantzissarantos Kh. - Kanellis   Chamois and Wild goats of Greece.
A.

First International Symposium for the Protection of Mediterranean monk - Rhodos 2-5
May 1978.

CONTENTS